Presented to

_____

on

_____

by

_____

_____

"Enter into the promises of God. It is your inheritance."
Smith Wigglesworth

SPIRITLED PROMISES FOR

Hope and Assurance

PASSIO
THE ART OF AUTHENTIC FAITH

Most CHARISMA HOUSE BOOK GROUP products are available at special quantity discounts for bulk purchase for sales promotions, premiums, fund-raising, and educational needs. For details, write Charisma House Book Group, 600 Rinehart Road, Lake Mary, Florida 32746, or telephone (407) 333-0600.

SPIRITLED PROMISES FOR HOPE AND ASSURANCE
Published by Passio
Charisma Media/Charisma House Book Group
600 Rinehart Road
Lake Mary, Florida 32746
www.charismahouse.com

Cover design by Lisa Rae Cox
Design Director: Bill Johnson

Library of Congress Control Number: 2013942020
International Standard Book Number: 978-1-62136-566-2
E-book ISBN: 978-1-62136-603-4

First edition

13 14 15 16 17 — 987654321
Printed in the United States of America

*Special thanks to Stanley M. Horton, ThD,
who served as the senior editorial advisor
for the Modern English Version, which is
used in SpiritLed Promises for Hope and
Assurance*

"Thanks be to God,
there is hope today;
this very hour
you can choose Him and serve Him."

D. L. MOODY

CONTENTS

INTRODUCTION

The future is as bright as the promises of God.
—ADONIRAM JUDSON

NO CHRISTIAN LIFE is complete without God's gift of hope and assurance. Hope is a virtue that results from a relationship with God through Christ. It isn't merely an emotion, something we might call hopefulness. Hope means having a life overflowing with pleasurable anticipation of a future filled with the assurance of joy and peace. It is waiting in confident expectation for God's promises in Christ to be graciously and powerfully fulfilled in our lives.

Hope is a vital necessity of our lives. It is a gift from our Creator that allows us to press on through life's challenges. It graces us with the ability to endure times and circumstances that would otherwise rob us of our joy and the life God has planned for us. Hope is knowing that God's grace will give you the strength for whatever you face and the assurance that nothing takes God by surprise. Hope gives us the courage we need to hold on.

Recalling the blessed hope of God's Word should give all believers the ability to confidently communicate what we know to be true even when present circumstances would point another direction. The objects of our hope are the spiritual blessings to which our eyes should be constantly directed. Our joy and peace resonate from our hope, and the greatest joy on earth is the hope of heaven. This hope of salvation is the most effective way of producing patience during our times of need.

Scripture is full of the promises of God, promises that help our faith and hope grow. No one scripture is more important or better than the rest, and each one joins the others to form an incredible picture of God's plan for our lives. Some verses will *challenge* the way we think. A few will *change* the way we think. And others may even change our lives.

This book is designed to help you be better acquainted with the power of God's Word. While the Bible has been around for a long time, the promises within have surprising relevance today. No one promise can stand alone without the support of every word God has provided. However, reading this collection of verses will help you better know which promise to stand on when seeking the hope you need and the assurance that God's mercy is His love of meeting our needs.

Today is your opportunity to fill your life with more wisdom, more happiness, and more assurance of God's love for you and His willingness to intervene in every area of your life. These promises have been selected for their power to transform your mind, heart, and soul so you can understand better, pray with purpose, grow your faith, and live with joy knowing God is the author of our hope and the finisher of His work.

> For all the promises of God in Him are "Yes," and in Him "Amen," to the glory of God through us.
>   —2 Corinthians 1:20

"Hope is a word which has taken on a new and deeper meaning for us because the Savior took it into His mouth. Loving Him and obeying Him, we suddenly discover that hope is really the direction taken by the whole Bible. Hope is the music of the whole Bible, the heartbeat, the pulse and the atmosphere of the whole Bible."

A. W. TOZER

Chapter 1

The Hope of Knowing God

The Love of God

The LORD did not set His love on you nor choose you because you were more in number than any of the peoples, for you were the fewest of all the peoples. But it is because the LORD loved you and because He kept the oath which He swore to your fathers. The LORD brought you out with a mighty hand and redeemed you out of the house of slavery, from the hand of Pharaoh, king of Egypt. Know therefore that the LORD your God, He is God, the faithful God, who keeps covenant and mercy with them who love Him and keep His commandments to a thousand generations.

—Deuteronomy 7:7–9

The Lord delighted only in your fathers, to love them; and He chose their descendants after them, even you above all people, as it is today.

—Deuteronomy 10:15

Your righteousness is like the great mountains; Your judgments like the great deep; O LORD, You preserve man and beast. How excellent is Your lovingkindness, O God! Therefore mankind seeks refuge in the shadow of Your wings.

—Psalm 36:6–7

But You, O Lord, are a God full of compassion and gracious, slow to anger, and abundant in mercy and truth.

—PSALM 86:15

The LORD opens the eyes of the blind; the LORD raises those who are brought down; the LORD loves the righteous.

—PSALM 146:8

The LORD has appeared to him from afar, saying, "Indeed, I have loved you with an everlasting love. Therefore with lovingkindness I have drawn you."

—JEREMIAH 31:3

For God so loved the world that He gave His only begotten Son, that whoever believes in Him should not perish, but have eternal life. For God did not send His Son into the world to condemn the world, but that the world through Him might be saved.

—JOHN 3:16–17

As the Father loved Me, I also loved you. Remain in My love.

—JOHN 15:9

And hope does not disappoint, because the love of God is shed abroad in our hearts by the Holy Spirit who has been given to us.

—ROMANS 5:5

Rarely for a righteous man will one die. Yet perhaps for a good man some would even dare to die. But God demonstrates His own love toward us, in that while we were yet sinners, Christ died for us.

—ROMANS 5:7–8

For as many as are led by the Spirit of God, these are the sons of God. For you have not received the spirit of slavery again to fear. But you have received the Spirit of adoption, by whom we cry, "Abba, Father." The Spirit Himself bears witness with our spirits that we are the children of God, and if children, then heirs: heirs of God and joint-heirs with Christ, if indeed we suffer with Him, that we may also be glorified with Him.

—ROMANS 8:14–17

Just as He chose us in Him before the foundation of the world, to be holy and blameless before Him in love, He predestined us to adoption as sons to Himself through Jesus Christ according to the good pleasure of His will, to the praise of the glory of His grace which He graciously bestowed on us in the Beloved.

—EPHESIANS 1:4–6

But God, being rich in mercy, because of His great love with which He loved us, even when we were dead in sins, made us alive together with Christ (by grace you have been saved), and He raised us up and seated us together in the heavenly places in Christ Jesus.

—Ephesians 2:4–6

And that Christ may dwell in your hearts through faith; that you, being rooted and grounded in love, may be able to comprehend with all saints what is the breadth and length and depth and height, and to know the love of Christ which surpasses knowledge; that you may be filled with all the fullness of God.

—Ephesians 3:17–19

Now may our Lord Jesus Christ Himself, and God our Father, who has loved us and has given us eternal consolation and good hope through grace…

—2 Thessalonians 2:16

Consider how much love the Father has given to us, that we should be called sons of God. Therefore the world does not know us, because it did not know Him.

—1 John 3:1

In this way the love of God was revealed to us, that God sent His only begotten Son into the world, that we might live through Him. In this is love: not that we loved God, but that He loved us and sent His Son to be the atoning sacrifice for our sins.

—1 John 4:9–10

We love Him because He first loved us.

—1 John 4:19

Grace, mercy, and peace will be with us from God the Father and from the Lord Jesus Christ, the Son of the Father, in truth and love.

—2 John 3

God's Love Is Compassionate

But after they had rest, they again did evil before You. Therefore You abandoned them to the hand of their enemies, so that they had dominion over them. Yet when they turned and cried to You, You heard from heaven, and many times You delivered them according to Your mercies.

—Nehemiah 9:28

For You, Lord, will bless the righteous. You surround him with favor like a shield.

—Psalm 5:12

He sent from above, He took me; He drew me out of many waters. He delivered me from my strong enemy, and from those who hated me, for they were too strong for me.

—Psalm 18:16–17

The eyes of the Lord are on the righteous, and His ears are open to their cry.

—Psalm 34:15

"But this shall be the covenant that I will make with the house of Israel after those days," says the Lord, "I will put My law within them and write it in their hearts. And will be their God, and they shall be My people. They shall teach no more every man his neighbor and every man his brother, saying, 'Know the Lord,' for they all shall know Me, from the least of them to the greatest of them," says the Lord, "for I will forgive their iniquity, and I will remember their sin no more."

—Jeremiah 31:33–34

I will take you for My wife forever. I will take you for My wife in righteousness and in justice, in mercy and in compassion.

—Hosea 2:19

I pulled them with cords of human kindness, with bands of love. I was to them as those who ease the yoke on their neck, and I bent down and fed them.

—Hosea 11:4

For as the body is one and has many parts, and all the many parts of that one body are one body, so also is Christ. For by one Spirit we are all baptized into one body, whether we are

Jews or Gentiles, whether we are slaves or free, and we have all been made to drink of one Spirit.

—1 Corinthians 12:12–13

Blessed be God, the Father of our Lord Jesus Christ, the Father of mercies, and the God of all comfort.

—2 Corinthians 1:3

For you know the grace of our Lord Jesus Christ, that though He was rich, yet for your sakes He became poor, that through His poverty you might be rich.

—2 Corinthians 8:9

God is able to make all grace abound toward you, so that you, always having enough of everything, may abound to every good work.

—2 Corinthians 9:8

But He said to me, "My grace is sufficient for you, for My strength is made perfect in weakness." Therefore most gladly I will boast in my weaknesses, that the power of Christ may rest upon me.

—2 Corinthians 12:9

And He raised us up and seated us together in the heavenly places in Christ Jesus, so that in the coming ages He might show the surpassing riches of His grace in kindness toward us in Christ Jesus.

—Ephesians 2:6–7

God's Love Offers Security

But may all those who seek refuge in You rejoice. May they ever shout for joy, because You defend them. May those who love Your name be joyful in You.

—Psalm 5:11

The Lord also will be a refuge for the oppressed, a refuge in times of trouble.

—Psalm 9:9

The Lord is the portion of my inheritance and of my cup; You support my lot. The lines have fallen for me in pleasant places; yes, an inheritance is beautiful for me.

—Psalm 16:5–6

I will bless the Lord who has given me counsel; my affections also instruct me in the night seasons. I have set the Lord always before me; because He is at my right hand, I will not be moved.

—Psalm 16:7–8

I love You, O Lord, my strength. The Lord is my pillar, and my fortress, and my deliverer; my God, my rock, in whom I take refuge; my shield, and the horn of my salvation, my high tower. I will call on the LORD, who is worthy to be praised, and I will be saved from my enemies.

—PSALM 18:1–3

May the LORD answer you in the day of trouble; may the name of the God of Jacob defend you.

—PSALM 20:1

For in the time of trouble He will hide me in His pavilion; in the shelter of His tabernacle He will hide me; He will set me up on a rock.

—PSALM 27:5

You are my hiding place; You will preserve me from trouble; You will surround me with shouts of deliverance.

—PSALM 32:7

God is our refuge and strength, a well-proven help in trouble.

—PSALM 46:1

I give them eternal life. They shall never perish, nor shall anyone snatch them from My hand.

—JOHN 10:28

GOD'S LOVE PROVIDES STRENGTH

My defense depends on God, who saves the upright in heart.

—Psalm 7:10

The Lord is my strength and my shield; my heart trusted in Him, and I was helped; therefore my heart rejoices, and with my song I will thank Him.

—Psalm 28:7

The Lord will give strength to His people; the Lord will bless His people with peace.

—Psalm 29:11

But the Lord loves justice, and does not forsake His saints.

—Psalm 37:28

What then shall we say to these things? If God is for us, who can be against us?

—Romans 8:31

GOD'S LOVE NEVER FAILS

Then you will prosper if you carefully observe the statutes and the judgments which the Lord commanded Moses for Israel.

—1 Chronicles 22:13

Many sorrows come to the wicked, but lovingkindness will surround the man who trusts in the LORD.

—PSALM 32:10

The eye of the LORD is on those who fear Him, on those who hope in His lovingkindness.

—PSALM 33:18

Your mercy, O LORD, is in the heavens, and Your faithfulness reaches to the clouds.

—PSALM 36:5

Yet the LORD will command His lovingkindness in the daytime, and in the night His song will be with me, a prayer to the God of my life.

—PSALM 42:8

I will sing of the mercies of the LORD forever; with my mouth I will make known Your faithfulness to all generations.

—PSALM 89:1

For the LORD is good; His mercy endures forever, and His faithfulness to all generations.

—PSALM 100:5

The LORD is near to all those who call upon Him, to all who call upon Him in truth.

—PSALM 145:18

And I prayed to the LORD my God, and made my confession, and said, "Alas, O Lord, the great and dreadful God, keeping His covenant and mercy to those who love Him, and to those who keep His commandments."

—DANIEL 9:4

Let your lives be without love of money, and be content with the things you have. For He has said, "I will never leave you, nor forsake you."

—HEBREWS 13:5

GOD'S LOVE IS COMFORTING

Those who know Your name will put their trust in You, for You, LORD, have not forsaken those who seek You.

—PSALM 9:10

Even though I walk through the valley of the shadow of death, I will fear no evil for You are with me; Your rod and Your staff they comfort me.

—PSALM 23:4

For the word of the LORD is upright, and all His work is done in truth. He loves righteousness and justice; the earth is full of the lovingkindness of the LORD.

—PSALM 33:4–5

The LORD is near to the brokenhearted, and saves the contrite of spirit. Many are the afflictions of the righteous, but the LORD delivers him out of them all.

—PSALM 34:18–19

But the salvation of the righteous is from the LORD; He is their refuge in the time of distress.

—PSALM 37:39

Come to Me, all you who labor and are heavily burdened, and I will give you rest.

—MATTHEW 11:28

Again, Jesus spoke to them, saying, "I am the light of the world. Whoever follows Me shall not walk in the darkness, but shall have the light of life."

—JOHN 8:12

And if I go and prepare a place for you, I will come again and receive you to Myself, that where I am, you may be also.

—JOHN 14:3

I will not leave you fatherless. I will come to you.

—JOHN 14:18

Blessed be God, the Father of our Lord Jesus Christ, the Father of mercies, and the God of all comfort, who comforts us in all our tribulation, that we may be able to comfort those who are in any trouble by the comfort with which we ourselves are comforted by God. As the sufferings of Christ abound in us, so our consolation also abounds through Christ.

—2 Corinthians 1:3–5

God's Love Is Ever Present

Oh, how great is Your goodness, which You have laid up for those who fear You, which You have done for those seeking refuge in You before people! You will hide them in the secret of Your presence from conspirators; You will keep them secretly in a shelter from the strife of tongues.

—Psalm 31:19–20

God is our refuge and strength, a well-proven help in trouble.

—Psalm 46:1

Teaching them to observe all things I have commanded you. And remember, I am with you always, even to the end of the age.

—Matthew 28:20

Who shall separate us from the love of Christ? Shall tribulation, or distress, or persecution, or famine, or nakedness, or peril, or sword? As it is written, "For Your sake we are killed all day long; we are counted as sheep for the slaughter." No, in all these things we are more than conquerors through Him who loved us. For I am persuaded that neither death nor life, neither angels nor principalities nor powers, neither things present nor things to come, neither height nor depth, nor any other created thing, shall be able to separate us from the love of God, which is in Christ Jesus our Lord.

—ROMANS 8:35–39

GOD'S LOVE SHOWS KINDNESS

Then David said to Solomon his son, "Be strong and courageous, and take action. Do not be afraid nor be dismayed for the LORD God, my God, is with you. He will not leave you nor forsake you, until you have finished all the work of the service of the house of the LORD."

—1 CHRONICLES 28:20

Show marvelously Your lovingkindness, O Deliverer of those who seek refuge by Your right hand from those who arise in opposition.

—PSALM 17:7

Remember Your mercies, O LORD, and Your lovingkindness, for they are from old. Do not remember the sins of my youth, or my transgressions; according to Your lovingkindness remember me, on account of Your goodness, O LORD.

—PSALM 25:6–7

I will be glad and rejoice in Your lovingkindness, for You have seen my trouble; You have known my soul in adversities.

—Psalm 31:7

The Lord is near to the brokenhearted; He saves the contrite of spirit.

—Psalm 34:18

Have mercy on me, O God, according to Your lovingkindness; according to the abundance of Your compassion, blot out my transgressions.

—Psalm 51:1

For I have said, "Mercy shall be built up forever; Your faithfulness shall be established in the heavens."

—Psalm 89:2

But the Lord takes pleasure in those who fear Him, in those who hope in His mercy.

—Psalm 147:11

Who is a God like You, bearing iniquity and passing over transgression for the remnant of His inheritance? He does not remain angry forever, because He delights in benevolence.

—Micah 7:18

In this is love: not that we loved God, but that He loved us and sent His Son to be the atoning sacrifice for our sins.

—1 John 4:10

GOD'S LOVE MEETS OUR NEEDS

The LORD is my shepherd; I shall not want.

—Psalm 23:1

The LORD is my strength and shield; my heart trusted in Him, and I was helped; therefore my heart rejoices, and with my song I will thank Him.

—Psalm 28:7

Delight yourself in the LORD, and He will give you the desires of your heart.

—Psalm 37:4

I have been young, and now am old; yet I have not seen the righteous forsaken, nor their offspring begging bread.

—Psalm 37:25

You will guide me with Your counsel, and afterward receive me to glory. Whom have I in heaven but You? And there is nothing on earth that I desire besides You. My flesh and my heart fails, but God is the strength of my heart and my portion forever.

—Psalm 73:24–26

For the Lord God is a sun and shield; the Lord will give favor and glory, for no good thing will He withhold from the one who walks uprightly.

—Psalm 84:11

The eyes of all wait upon You, and You give them their food in due season. You open Your hand and satisfy the desire of every living thing.

—Psalm 145:15–16

O Lord, You who know, remember me, and take notice of me, and take vengeance on my persecutors. Because of your longsuffering, do not take me away. Know that for Your sake I have suffered rebuke.

—Jeremiah 15:15

Behold, I am the Lord, the God of all flesh. Is anything too hard for Me?

—Jeremiah 32:27

I will make them and the places round about My hill a blessing. And I will cause the showers to come down in their season. They shall be showers of blessing. The tree of the field shall yield its fruit, and the ground shall yield its increase, and they shall be safe in their land. Then they shall know that I am the Lord, when I have broken the

bands of their yoke and delivered them out of the hand of
those who enslaved them.

—EZEKIEL 34:26–27

If you remain in Me, and My words remain in you, you will
ask whatever you desire, and it shall be done for you.

—JOHN 15:7

Yet He did not leave Himself without witness, for He did
good and gave us rain from heaven and fruitful seasons, sat-
isfying our hearts with food and gladness.

—ACTS 14:17

For He says, "In an acceptable time I have listened to you,
and in the day of salvation I have helped you." Look, now is
the accepted time; look, now is the day of salvation.

—2 CORINTHIANS 6:2

But my God shall supply your every need according to His
riches in glory by Christ Jesus.

—PHILIPPIANS 4:19

Command those who are rich in this world that they not
be conceited, nor trust in uncertain riches, but in the living
God, who richly gives us all things to enjoy.

—1 TIMOTHY 6:17

GOD'S LOVE PROVIDES FORGIVENESS

They refused to obey and were not mindful of Your wonders that You performed among them. But they hardened their necks and in their rebellion appointed a leader to return to their bondage. But, You are a God ready to pardon, gracious and merciful, slow to anger and abounding in kindness, and did not forsake them.

—NEHEMIAH 9:17

Hide Your face from my sins, and blot out all my iniquities. Create in me a clean heart, O God, and renew a right spirit within me.

—PSALM 51:9–10

Bless the LORD, O my soul, and forget not all His benefits, who forgives all your iniquities, who heals all your diseases.

—PSALM 103:2–3

He who covers his sins will not prosper, but whoever confesses and forsakes them will have mercy.

—PROVERBS 28:13

"They shall teach no more every man his neighbor and every man his brother, saying, 'Know the LORD,' for they all shall know Me, from the least of them to the greatest of them," said the LORD. "For I will forgive their sin and I will remember their offense no more."

—JEREMIAH 31:34

For this is My blood of the new covenant, which is shed for many for the remission of sins.

—MATTHEW 26:28

Therefore repent and be converted, that your sins may be wiped away, that times of refreshing may come from the presence of the Lord.

—ACTS 3:19

Therefore, if any man is in Christ, he is a new creature. Old things have passed away. Look, all things have become new.

—2 CORINTHIANS 5:17

In Him we have redemption through His blood and the forgiveness of sins according to the riches of His grace.

—EPHESIANS 1:7

But if we walk in the light as He is in the light, we have fellowship one with another, and the blood of Jesus Christ His Son cleanses us from all sin. If we say that we have no sin, we deceive ourselves, and the truth is not in us. If we confess our sins, He is faithful and just to forgive us our sins and cleanse us from all unrighteousness.

—1 JOHN 1:7–9

GOD'S LOVE CONQUERS FEAR

I will both lie down in peace and sleep; for You, Lord, make me dwell safely and securely.

—Psalm 4:8

Peace I leave with you. My peace I give to you. Not as the world gives do I give to you. Let not your heart be troubled, neither let it be afraid.

—John 14:27

For you have not received the spirit of slavery again to fear. But you have received the Spirit of adoption, by whom we cry, "Abba, Father."

—Romans 8:15

We know that all things work together for good to those who love God, to those who are called according to His purpose.... What then shall we say to these things? If God is for us, who can be against us? He who did not spare His own Son, but delivered Him up for us all, how shall He not with Him also freely give us all things?

—Romans 8:28, 31–32

There is no fear in love, but perfect love casts out fear, because fear has to do with punishment. Whoever fears is not perfect in love.

—1 John 4:18

GOD AND HIS LOVE ARE SOVEREIGN

The LORD will reign forever and ever.

—EXODUS 15:18

For the LORD your God is the God of gods and Lord of lords, the great, the mighty, and the fearsome God who is unbiased, and takes no bribe.

—DEUTERONOMY 10:17

Our hearts melted when we heard these things, and no man had any breath in him because of you, for the LORD your God is God in heaven above and on earth below.

—JOSHUA 2:11

For great is the LORD and greatly to be praised. He is to be feared above all other gods.

—1 CHRONICLES 16:25

Then the LORD answered Job out of the whirlwind and said: "Who is this who darkens council by words without knowledge?"

—JOB 38:1–2

The earth belongs to the LORD, and its fullness, the world, and those who dwell in it.

—PSALM 24:1

That they may know that You, whose name alone is the LORD, are the Most High over all the earth.

—PSALM 83:18

For You, O LORD, are Most High above all the earth; You are exalted far above all gods.

—PSALM 97:9

The LORD is righteous in all His ways and loving in all His works.

—PSALM 145:17

Thus said the LORD, the King of Israel, and his Redeemer the LORD of Hosts. "I am the first, and I am the last. And beside Me there is no God."

—ISAIAH 44:6

There was given to him dominion, and glory, and a kingdom, that all peoples, nations, and languages, should serve him. His dominion is an everlasting dominion, which shall not pass away, and his kingdom that which shall not be destroyed.

—DANIEL 7:14

Then the kingdom and dominion, and the greatness of all the kingdoms under the whole heaven, shall be given to the people of the saints of the Most High, whose kingdom is an everlasting kingdom, and all dominions shall serve and obey him.

—Daniel 7:27

This righteousness of God comes through faith in Jesus Christ to all and upon all who believe, for there is no distinction.

—Romans 3:22

Which He, who is the blessed and only Ruler, the King of kings and Lord of lords, will reveal at the proper time.

—1 Timothy 6:15

"I am the Alpha and the Omega, the Beginning and the End," says the Lord, "who is and who was and who is to come, the Almighty."

—Revelation 1:8

GOD'S LOVE BRINGS PEACE

Blessed are all who seek refuge in Him.

—Psalm 2:12

Let not your heart be troubled. You believe in God. Believe also in Me. In My Father's house are many dwelling places. If it were not so, I would have told you. I am going to prepare a place for you. And if I go and prepare a place for you,

I will come again and receive you to Myself, that where I am, you may be also.

—John 14:1–3

To be carnally minded is death, but to be spiritually minded is life and peace.

—Romans 8:6

Let the peace of God, to which also you are called in one body, rule in your hearts. And be thankful.

—Colossians 3:15

Now may the Lord of peace Himself give you peace always in every way. The Lord be with you all.

—2 Thessalonians 3:16

GOD'S LOVE IS JUST

The Lord, the Lord God, merciful and gracious, slow to anger, and abounding in goodness and truth, Keeping mercy for thousands, forgiving iniquity and transgression and sin, but who will by no means clear the guilty, visiting the iniquity of fathers on the children and on the children's children, to the third and fourth generation.

—Exodus 34:6–7

If you listen to these judgments, keep them, and do them, then the Lord your God shall keep with you the covenant and the mercy which He swore to your fathers. He will love you and bless you and multiply you. He will also bless the fruit of your womb and the fruit of your land, your corn, and your wine, and your oil, the increase of your herd and the young of your flock, in the land which He swore to your fathers to give you.

—Deuteronomy 7:12–13

O Lord God of heaven, the great and awesome God, who keeps covenant and mercy for those who love Him and keep His commandments. Let Your ear now be attentive, and Your eyes open, that You may hear the prayer of Your servant.

—Nehemiah 1:5–6

It is of the Lord's mercies that we are not consumed, because His compassions do not fail. They are new every morning. Great is Your faithfulness. "The Lord is my portion," says my soul, "Therefore I will hope in Him."

—Lamentations 3:22–24

The Lord is good, a stronghold in a day of distress. He knows those who take refuge in Him.

—Nahum 1:7

"*Many things are possible for the person who has hope. Even more is possible for the person who has faith. And still more is possible for the person who knows how to love. But everything is possible for the person who practices all three virtues.*"

BROTHER LAWRENCE

Chapter 2

LIVING THE CHRISTIAN LIFE

LIVING WITH HOPE

Lead me in Your truth and teach me, for You are the God of my salvation; on You I wait all day long.

—PSALM 25:5

Wait for the LORD; be strong, and may your heart be stout; wait on the LORD.

—PSALM 27:14

Our soul waits for the LORD; He is our help and our shield.

—PSALM 33:20

Let Your lovingkindness, O LORD, be on us, just as we hope in You.

—PSALM 33:22

Why are you cast down, O my soul? And why are you disquieted within me? Hope in God; for I will yet give Him thanks, the salvation of my countenance and my God.

—PSALM 43:5

God is our refuge and strength, a well-proven help in trouble.

—PSALM 46:1

My soul, wait silently for God, for my hope is from Him. He only is my rock and my salvation; He is my refuge; I will not be moved.

—Psalm 62:5–6

For You are my hope, O Lord God; You are my confidence from my youth.

—Psalm 71:5

You who fear the Lord, trust in the Lord; He is their help and their shield.

—Psalm 115:11

My soul longs for Your deliverance, but I hope in Your word.

—Psalm 119:81

I wait for the Lord, with bated breath I wait; I long for His Word!

—Psalm 130:5

Let Israel wait for the Lord! For mercy is found with the Lord; with Him is great redemption.

—Psalm 130:7

Blessed is the one who has the God of Jacob for his help, whose hope is in the Lord his God, who made heaven, and earth, the sea, and all that is in them, who keeps faithfulness forever.

—Psalm 146:5–6

Hope deferred makes the heart sick, but when the desire comes, it is a tree of life.

—Proverbs 13:12

But as for me, I watch for the Lord, I await the God of my salvation—my God will hear me. Do not rejoice over me, my enemy! Although I have fallen, I will rise. Although I dwell in darkness, the Lord is my light!

—Micah 7:7–8

What then shall we say to these things? If God is for us, who can be against us? He who did not spare His own Son, but delivered Him up for us all, how shall He not with Him also freely give us all things? Who shall bring a charge against God's elect? It is God who justifies.

—Romans 8:31–33

That the eyes of your heart may be enlightened, that you may know what is the hope of His calling and what are the riches of the glory of His inheritance among the saints.

—Ephesians 1:18

And be found in Him, not having my own righteousness which is from the law, but that which is through faith in

Christ, the righteousness which is of God on the basis of faith, to know Him, and the power of His resurrection, and the fellowship of His sufferings, being conformed to His death, if somehow I might make it to the resurrection of the dead.

—Philippians 3:9–11

As we await the blessed hope and the appearing of the glory of our great God and Savior Jesus Christ.

—Titus 2:13

We desire that every one of you show the same diligence for the full assurance of hope to the end, so that you may not be lazy, but imitators of those who through faith and patience inherit the promises.

—Hebrews 6:11–12

So that by two immutable things, in which it was impossible for God to lie, we who have fled for refuge might have strong encouragement to hold fast to the hope set before us. We have this hope as a sure and steadfast anchor of the soul, which enters the Inner Place behind the veil.

—Hebrews 6:18–19

Blessed be the God and Father of our Lord Jesus Christ, who according to His abundant mercy has given us a new birth into a living hope through the resurrection of Jesus Christ from the dead.

—1 Peter 1:3

But sanctify the Lord God in your hearts. Always be ready to give an answer to every man who asks you for a reason for the hope that is in you, with gentleness and fear.

—1 Peter 3:15

Beloved, now are we sons of God, and it has not yet been revealed what we shall be. But we know that when He appears, we shall be like Him, for we shall see Him as He is. Everyone who has this hope in Him purifies himself, just as He is pure.

—1 John 3:2–3

Living With Faith

Ask and it will be given to you; seek and you will find; knock and it will be opened to you. For everyone who asks receives, and he who seeks finds, and to him who knocks, it will be opened.

—Matthew 7:7–8

Jesus said to them, "Because of your unbelief. For truly I say to you, if you have faith as a grain of mustard seed, you will say to this mountain, 'Move from here to there,' and it will move. And nothing will be impossible for you."

—Matthew 17:20

Jesus said, "If you can believe! All things are possible to him who believes."

—Mark 9:23

Jesus answered them, "Have faith in God. For truly I say to you, whoever says to this mountain, 'Be removed and be thrown into the sea,' and does not doubt in his heart, but believes that what he says will come to pass, he will have whatever he says. Therefore I say to you, whatever things you ask when you pray, believe that you will receive them, and you will have them."

—Mark 11:22–24

Jesus said to him, "Thomas, because you have seen Me, you have believed. Blessed are those who have not seen, and have yet believed."

—John 20:29

For in it the righteousness of God is revealed from faith to faith. As it is written, "The just shall live by faith."

—Romans 1:17

What then shall we say to these things? If God is for us, who can be against us? He who did not spare His own Son, but delivered Him up for us all, how shall He not with Him also freely give us all things?

—Romans 8:31–32

So then faith comes by hearing, and hearing by the word of God.

—Romans 10:17

But as it is written, "Eye has not seen, nor ear heard, neither has it entered into the heart of man, the things which God has prepared for those who love Him."

—1 Corinthians 2:9

But we have this treasure in earthen vessels, the excellency of the power being from God and not from ourselves.

—2 Corinthians 4:7

We are troubled on every side, yet not distressed; we are perplexed, but not in despair; persecuted, but not forsaken; cast down, but not destroyed.

—2 Corinthians 4:8–9

For this reason we do not lose heart: Even though our outward man is perishing, yet our inward man is being renewed day by day. Our light affliction, which lasts but for a moment, works for us a far more exceeding and eternal weight of glory, while we do not look at the things which are seen, but at the things which are not seen. For the things which are seen are temporal, but the things which are not seen are eternal.

—2 Corinthians 4:16–18

For we walk by faith, not by sight.

—2 Corinthians 5:7

I have fought a good fight, I have finished my course, and I have kept the faith. From now on a crown of righteousness is laid up for me, which the Lord, the righteous Judge, will give me on that Day, and not only to me but also to all who have loved His appearing.

—2 Timothy 4:7–8

Let us draw near with a true heart in full assurance of faith, having our hearts sprinkled to cleanse them from an evil conscience, and our bodies washed with pure water.

—Hebrews 10:22

Let us firmly hold the profession of our faith without wavering, for He who promised is faithful.

—Hebrews 10:23

Therefore do not throw away your confidence, which will be greatly rewarded.

—Hebrews 10:35

Now faith is the substance of things hoped for, the evidence of things not seen....By faith we understand that the universe was framed by the word of God, so that things that are seen were not made out of things which are visible....And without faith it is impossible to please God, for he who comes to God must believe that He exists and that He is a rewarder of those who diligently seek Him.

—Hebrews 11:1, 3, 6

Let us look to Jesus, the author and finisher of our faith, who for the joy that was set before Him endured the cross, despising the shame, and is seated at the right hand of the throne of God.

—Hebrews 12:2

Whom, having not seen, you love; and in whom, though you do not see Him now, you believe and you rejoice with joy unspeakable and full of glory, receiving as the result of your faith the salvation of your souls.

—1 Peter 1:8–9

This is the confidence that we have in Him, that if we ask anything according to His will, He hears us. So if we know that He hears whatever we ask, we know that we have whatever we asked of Him.

—1 John 5:14–15

LIVING WITH LOVE

Hatred stirs up strife, but love covers all sins.

—PROVERBS 10:12

You have heard that it was said, "You shall love your neighbor and hate your enemy." But I say to you, love your enemies, bless those who curse you, do good to those who hate you, and pray for those who spitefully use you and persecute you.

—MATTHEW 5:43–44

A new commandment I give to you, that you love one another, even as I have loved you, that you also love one another. By this all men will know that you are My disciples, if you have love for one another.

—JOHN 13:34–35

For the Father Himself loves you, because you have loved Me, and have believed that I came from God.

—JOHN 16:27

While we were yet weak, in due time Christ died for the ungodly....But God demonstrates His own love toward us, in that while we were yet sinners, Christ died for us.

—ROMANS 5:6, 8

Love works no evil to a neighbor. Therefore love is the fulfillment of the law. Furthermore, knowing the time, now is the moment to awake from sleep. For now our salvation is nearer than when we believed.

—ROMANS 13:10–11

In whom we have boldness and confident access through faith in Him.

—EPHESIANS 3:12

And this I pray, that your love may abound yet more and more in knowledge and in all discernment, that you may approve things that are excellent so that you may be pure and blameless for the day of Christ.

—PHILIPPIANS 1:9–10

Then fulfill my joy and be like-minded, having the same love, being in unity with one mind.

—PHILIPPIANS 2:2

So flee youthful desires and pursue righteousness, faith, love, and peace, with those who call on the Lord out of a pure heart.

—2 TIMOTHY 2:22

If you fulfill the royal law according to the Scripture, "You shall love your neighbor as yourself," you are doing well.

—JAMES 2:8

Finally, be all of one mind, be loving toward one another, be gracious, and be kind.

—1 Peter 3:8

Above all things, have unfailing love for one another, because love covers a multitude of sins.

—1 Peter 4:8

For this reason, make every effort to add virtue to your faith; and to your virtue, knowledge; and to your knowledge, self-control; and to your self-control, patient endurance; and to your patient endurance, godliness; and to your godliness, brotherly kindness; and to your brotherly kindness, love.

—2 Peter 1:5–7

But whoever keeps His word truly has the love of God perfected in him. By this we know we are in Him.

—1 John 2:5

Whoever loves his brother lives in the light, and in him there is no cause for stumbling.

—1 John 2:10

Beloved, let us love one another, for love is of God, and everyone who loves is born of God and knows God. Anyone who does not love does not know God, for God is love. In this way the love of God was revealed to us, that God sent

His only begotten Son into the world, that we might live through Him. In this is love: not that we loved God, but that He loved us and sent His Son to be the atoning sacrifice for our sins. Beloved, if God so loved us, we must also love one another.

—1 JOHN 4:7–11

And we have come to know and to believe the love that God has for us. God is love. Whoever lives in love lives in God, and God in him.

—1 JOHN 4:16

If anyone says, "I love God," and hates his brother, he is a liar. For whoever does not love his brother whom he has seen, how can he love God whom he has not seen? We have this commandment from Him: Whoever loves God must also love his brother.

—1 JOHN 4:20–21

And this is love: that we walk according to His commandments. This is the commandment, that as you have heard from the beginning, you should walk in it.

—2 JOHN 6

LIVING IN PRAYER

Depart from me, all you workers of iniquity; for the Lord has heard the voice of my weeping. The Lord has heard my supplication; the Lord accepts my prayer.

—Psalm 6:8–9

The eyes of the Lord are on the righteous, and His ears are open to their cry. The face of the Lord is against the ones doing evil, to cut off the memory of them from the earth.

—Psalm 34:15–16

For in You, O Lord, do I hope; You will answer, O Lord my God.

—Psalm 38:15

Evening and morning and at noon, I will make my complaint and murmur, and He will hear my voice.

—Psalm 55:17

I will mention the steadfast love of the Lord and the praises of the Lord, according to all that the Lord has bestowed on us, and the great goodness toward the house of Israel, which He has bestowed on them according to His mercy, and according to the multitude of His kindnesses.

—Isaiah 63:7

Call to Me, and I will answer you, and show you great and mighty things which you do not know.

—JEREMIAH 33:3

Now when Daniel knew that the writing was signed, he went into his house. And his windows being open in his chamber toward Jerusalem, he kneeled on his knees three times a day, and prayed, and gave thanks before his God, as he had been doing previously.

—DANIEL 6:10

When you pray, you shall not be like the hypocrites. For they love to pray standing in the synagogues and on the street corners that they may be seen by men. Truly I say to you, they have their reward. But you, when you pray, enter your closet, and when you have shut your door, pray to your Father who is in secret. And your Father who sees in secret will reward you openly.

—MATTHEW 6:5–6

Again I say to you, that if two of you agree on earth about anything they ask, it will be done for them by My Father who is in heaven. For where two or three are assembled in My name, there I am in their midst.

—MATTHEW 18:19–20

Therefore I say to you, whatever things you ask when you pray, believe that you will receive them, and you will have them. And when you stand praying, forgive if you have anything against anyone, so that your Father who is in heaven may also forgive you your sins.

—Mark 11:24–25

But I say to you who hear, love your enemies, do good to those who hate you, bless those who curse you, and pray for those who spitefully use you.

—Luke 6:27–28

I will do whatever you ask in My name, that the Father may be glorified in the Son. If you ask anything in My name, I will do it.

—John 14:13–14

Now I ask you, brothers, through the Lord Jesus Christ and through the love of the Spirit, to strive together with me in your prayers to God on my behalf.

—Romans 15:30

Therefore I exhort first of all that you make supplications, prayers, intercessions, and thanksgivings for everyone.... Therefore I desire that the men pray everywhere, lifting up holy hands, without wrath or contentiousness.

—1 Timothy 2:1, 8

Is anyone among you suffering? Let him pray. Is anyone merry? Let him sing psalms. Is anyone sick among you?

Let him call for the elders of the church, and let them pray over him, anointing him with oil in the name of the Lord. And the prayer of faith will save the sick, and the Lord will raise him up. And if he has committed any sins, he will be forgiven. Confess your faults to one another and pray for one another, that you may be healed. The effective, fervent prayer of a righteous man accomplishes much.

James 5:13–16

For the eyes of the Lord are on the righteous, and His ears are open to their prayers, but the face of the Lord is against those who do evil.

—1 Peter 3:12

Living in Obedience

Blessed are those who keep His testimonies, who seek Him with all their heart.

—Psalm 119:2

I consider my ways, and I turn my feet to Your testimonies. I made haste, and I did not delay to keep Your commandments.

—Psalm 119:59–60

He who keeps the commandment keeps his own soul, but he who is careless in his ways will die.

—Proverbs 19:16

But this thing I commanded them, saying, "Obey My voice, and I will be your God, and you shall be My people. And walk in all the ways that I have commanded you, that it may be well with you."

—Jeremiah 7:23

Obey My voice, and do according to all which I command you. So you shall be My people, and I will be your God.

—Jeremiah 11:4

Whoever comes to Me and hears My words and does them, I will show whom he is like: He is like a man who built a house, and dug deep, and laid the foundation on rock. When the flood arose, the stream beat vehemently against that house, but could not shake it, for it was founded on rock.

—Luke 6:47–48

But He said, "Indeed, blessed are those who hear the word of God and keep it."

—Luke 11:28

Jesus answered him, "If a man loves Me, he will keep My word. My Father will love him, and We will come to him, and make Our home with him. He who does not love Me does not keep My words. The word which you hear is not Mine, but the Father's who sent Me."

—John 14:23–24

If you keep My commandments, you will remain in My love, even as I have kept My Father's commandments and remain in His love. I have spoken these things to you, that My joy may remain in you, and that your joy may be full.

—John 15:10–11

Peter and the other apostles answered, "We must obey God rather than men."

—Acts 5:29

Circumcision is nothing, and uncircumcision is nothing, but the keeping of the commandments of God is everything.... You were bought at a price. Do not be the servants of men.

—1 Corinthians 7:19, 23

I say then, walk in the Spirit, and you shall not fulfill the lust of the flesh.

—Galatians 5:16

This is a faithful saying: "If we die with Him, we shall also live with Him," "If we endure, we shall also reign with Him; if we deny Him, He also will deny us."

—2 Timothy 2:11–12

Be doers of the word and not hearers only, deceiving yourselves. For if anyone is a hearer of the word and not a doer, he is like a man viewing his natural face in a mirror. He views himself, and goes his way, and immediately forgets what kind of man he was.

—James 1:22–24

Beloved, if our heart does not condemn us, then we have confidence before God. And whatever we ask, we will receive from Him, because we keep His commandments and do the things that are pleasing in His sight.

—1 John 3:21–22

LIVING IN PRAISE AND WORSHIP

This book of the law must not depart from your mouth. Meditate on it day and night so that you may act carefully according to all that is written in it. For then you will make your way successful, and you will be wise. Have not I commanded you? Be strong and courageous. Do not be afraid or dismayed, for the Lord your God is with you wherever you go.

—Joshua 1:8–9

I love you, O Lord, my strength.

—Psalm 18:1

The law of the Lord is perfect, converting the soul. The testimony of the Lord is sure, making wise the simple. The statutes of the Lord are right, rejoicing the heart. The commandment of the Lord is pure, enlightening the eyes.... More to be desired are they than gold, yes, than much fine gold; sweeter also than honey and the honeycomb.

—Psalm 19:7–8, 10

One thing I have asked from the Lord, that will I seek after—for me to dwell in the house of the Lord all the days of my life, to see the beauty of the Lord, and to inquire in His temple.

—Psalm 27:4

Give to the Lord, you heavenly beings, give to the Lord glory and strength. Give to the Lord the glory of His name; worship the Lord in holy splendor.

—Psalm 29:1–2

Sing to the Lord, O you saints of His, and give thanks at the remembrance of His holiness.

—Psalm 30:4

Thus will I bless You while I live; I will lift up my hands in Your name.

—Psalm 63:4

O come, let us worship and bow down; let us kneel before the Lord, our Maker. For He is our God, and we are the people of His pasture and the sheep of His hand. Today if you hear His voice, do not harden your hearts, as at Meribah, and as in the day of Massah in the wilderness.

—Psalm 95:6–8

O give thanks unto the Lord; call upon His name; make known His deeds among the peoples. Sing unto Him, sing praises unto Him; proclaim all His wondrous works.

—Psalm 105:1–2

Praise the Lord! O give thanks unto the Lord, for He is good, for His mercy endures forever. Who can recount the mighty acts of the Lord or declare all His praise?

—Psalm 106:1–2

From the rising of the sun to its going down, the Lord's name is to be praised.

—Psalm 113:3

Bow your heavens, O Lord, and come down; touch the mountains, and they shall smoke.

—Psalm 144:5

Every day will I bless You, I will praise Your name forever and ever.

—Psalm 145:2

Sing unto the LORD a new song, and His praise in the assembly of the godly ones.

—PSALM 149:1

A merry heart makes a cheerful countenance, but by sorrow of the heart the spirit is broken.

—PROVERBS 15:13

Give her of the fruit of her hands, and let her own works praise her in the gates.

—PROVERBS 31:31

Thus says the LORD, "Again there shall be heard in this place of which you say, 'It is desolate, without man and without beast,' even in the cities of Judah, and in the streets of Jerusalem, that are desolate, without man and without inhabitant, and without beast, the voice of joy, and the voice of gladness, the voice of the bridegroom, and the voice of the bride, the voice of those who shall say, 'Give thanks to the LORD of Hosts, for the LORD is good. For His mercy endures forever,' and of those who bring the sacrifice of praise into the house of the LORD. For I will restore the fortunes of the land as at the first," says the LORD.

—JEREMIAH 33:10–11

Yet the hour is coming, and is now here, when the true worshippers will worship the Father in spirit and truth. For the

Father seeks such to worship Him. God is Spirit and those who worship Him must worship Him in spirit and truth.

—JOHN 4:23–24

Blessed be the God and Father of our Lord Jesus Christ, who has blessed us with every spiritual blessing in the heavenly places in Christ.

—EPHESIANS 1:3

Chapter 3

Living Like Jesus

Called to Love

And you shall love the LORD your God, with all your heart and with all your soul and with all your might.

—Deuteronomy 6:5

What I am commanding you today is to love the LORD your God, to walk in His ways, and to keep His commandments and His statutes and His judgments, so that you may live and multiply. Then the LORD your God will bless you in the land which you go to possess.

—Deuteronomy 30:16

By loving the LORD your God and obeying His voice and clinging to Him. For He is your life and the length of your days, so that you may dwell in the land which the LORD swore to your fathers, to Abraham, to Isaac, and to Jacob, to give them.

—Deuteronomy 30:20

Only carefully obey the commandment and the law that Moses the servant of the LORD commanded you: to love the LORD your God, to walk in all His ways, to obey His commandments, to cling to Him, and to serve Him with all your heart and soul.

—Joshua 22:5

Now be careful, therefore, to love the Lord your God!

—Joshua 23:11

Oh, love the Lord, all you His saints, for the Lord preserves the faithful, but amply repays the one who acts in pride.

—Psalm 31:23

He answered, "'You shall love the Lord your God with all your heart, and with all your soul, and with all your strength, and with all your mind' and 'your neighbor as yourself.'"

—Luke 10:27

Greater love has no man than this: that a man lay down his life for his friends.

—John 15:13

Owe no one anything, except to love one another, for he who loves another has fulfilled the law. For the commandments, "You shall not commit adultery, You shall not kill, You shall not steal, You shall not bear false witness, You shall not covet," and if there are any other commandments, are summed up in this saying, "You shall love your neighbor as yourself." Love works no evil to a neighbor. Therefore love is the fulfillment of the law.

—ROMANS 13:8–10

God is faithful, and by Him you were called to the fellowship of His Son, Jesus Christ our Lord.

—1 CORINTHIANS 1:9

But God has chosen the foolish things of the world to confound the wise. God has chosen the weak things of the world to confound the things which are mighty. And God has chosen the base things of the world and things which are despised. Yes, and He chose things which did not exist to bring to nothing things that do, so that no flesh should boast in His presence.

—1 CORINTHIANS 1:27–29

For the entire law is fulfilled in one word, even in this: "You shall love your neighbor as yourself."

—GALATIANS 5:14

I thank my God for every reminder of you. In every prayer of mine for you all, I have always made requests with joy, due to your fellowship in the gospel from the first day until now.

—PHILIPPIANS 1:3–5

And may the Lord make you increase and abound in love for one another and for all men, even as we do for you.

—1 Thessalonians 3:12

As concerning brotherly love, you do not need me to write to you. For you yourselves are taught by God to love one another.

—1 Thessalonians 4:9

We ask you, brothers, to acknowledge those who labor among you, and are appointed over you in the Lord, and instruct you. Esteem them very highly in love for their work's sake. And be at peace among yourselves.

—1 Thessalonians 5:12–13

We are bound to thank God always for you, brothers, as it is fitting, because your faith is growing abundantly, and the love of every one of you abounds toward each other.

—2 Thessalonians 1:3

Let brotherly love continue.

—Hebrews 13:1

Since your souls have been purified by obedience to the truth through the Spirit unto a genuine brotherly love, love one another deeply with a pure heart.

—1 Peter 1:22

Honor all people. Love the brotherhood. Fear God. Honor
the king.

—1 PETER 2:17

For this is the message that you heard from the beginning:
We should love one another.

—1 JOHN 3:11

Beloved, if God so loved us, we must also love one another.
No one has seen God at any time. If we love one another,
God dwells in us, and His love is perfected in us.

—1 JOHN 4:11–12

We have this commandment from Him: Whoever loves
God must also love his brother.

—1 JOHN 4:21

CALLED TO HOLINESS

Consecrate yourselves therefore, and be holy, for I am the
LORD your God. You shall keep My statutes, and do them;
I am the LORD who sanctifies you.

—LEVITICUS 20:7–8

All the paths of the LORD are lovingkindness and truth, for
those who keep His covenant and His testimonies.

—PSALM 25:10

Blessed be the Lord, who daily loads us with benefits, even the God who is our salvation.

—Psalm 68:19

The light of the eyes rejoices the heart, and a good report makes the bones healthy.

—Proverbs 15:30

He who follows after righteousness and mercy finds life, righteousness, and honor.

—Proverbs 21:21

In the morning sow your seed, and in the evening do not let your hand rest, because you do not know which activity will find success, this way or that way, or if both will be good.

—Ecclesiastes 11:6

Therefore be perfect, even as your Father who is in heaven is perfect.

—Matthew 5:48

But seek first the kingdom of God and His righteousness, and all these things shall be given to you.

—Matthew 6:33

"The essence of optimism is that it takes no account of the present, but it is a source of inspiration, of vitality and hope where others have resigned; it enables a man to hold his head high, to claim the future for himself and not to abandon it to his enemy."

DIETRICH BONHOEFFER

Jesus said to him, "If you would be perfect, go and sell what you have, and give to the poor, and you will have treasure in heaven. And come, follow Me."

—Matthew 19:21

Let love be without hypocrisy. Hate what is evil. Cleave to what is good.

—Romans 12:9

Since we have these promises, beloved, let us cleanse ourselves from all filthiness of the flesh and spirit, perfecting holiness in the fear of God.

—2 Corinthians 7:1

Not that I have already attained or have already been perfected, but I follow after it so that I may lay hold of that for which I was seized by Christ Jesus.

—Philippians 3:12

To this end may He establish your hearts to be blameless in holiness before our God and Father at the coming of our Lord Jesus Christ with all His saints.

—1 Thessalonians 3:13

For God has not called us to uncleanness, but to holiness.

—1 Thessalonians 4:7

But you, O man of God, escape these things, and follow after righteousness, godliness, faith, love, patience, and gentleness.

—1 Timothy 6:11

Now may the God of peace, who through the blood of the eternal covenant brought again from the dead our Lord Jesus, the Great Shepherd of the sheep, make you perfect in every good work to do His will, working in you that which is pleasing in His sight, through Jesus Christ, to whom be glory forever and ever. Amen.

—Hebrews 13:20–21

Called to Be Content

David replied to Gad, "I am in great distress. Let me fall into the hands of the LORD, for His mercies are very great, but do not let me fall into the hand of men."

—1 Chronicles 21:13

Rest in the LORD, and wait patiently for Him; do not fret because of those who prosper in their way, because of those who make wicked schemes. Let go of anger, and forsake wrath; do not fret—it surely leads to evil deeds.

—Psalm 37:7–8

Make a joyful noise unto the LORD, all the earth! Serve the LORD with gladness; come before His presence with singing.

Know that the LORD, He is God. It is He who has made us, and not we ourselves; we are His people, and the sheep of His pasture.

—PSALM 100:1–3

I will greatly rejoice in the LORD, my soul shall be joyful in my God. For He has clothed me with the garments of salvation. He has covered me with the robe of righteousness, as a bridegroom decks himself with ornaments, and as a bride adorns herself with her jewels.

—ISAIAH 61:10

Though the fig tree does not blossom, nor fruit be on the vines; though the yield of the olive fails and the fields produce no food; though the flocks are cut off from the fold, and no cattle are in the stalls, yet I will rejoice in the LORD; I will exult in the God of my salvation.

—HABAKKUK 3:17–18

Do not store up for yourselves treasures on earth where moth and rust destroy and where thieves break in and steal. But store up for yourselves treasures in heaven, where neither moth nor rust destroy and where thieves do not break in nor steal, for where your treasure is, there will your heart be also.

—MATTHEW 6:19–21

For he who serves Christ in these things is acceptable to God and approved by men. Therefore let us pursue the things which produce peace and the things that build up one another.

—Romans 14:18–19

Be anxious for nothing, but in everything, by prayer and supplication with gratitude, make your requests known to God. And the peace of God, which surpasses all understanding, will protect your hearts and minds through Christ Jesus.

—Philippians 4:6–7

I do not speak because I have need, for I have learned in whatever state I am to be content. I know both how to face humble circumstances and how to have abundance. Everywhere and in all things I have learned the secret, both to be full and to be hungry, both to abound and to suffer need. I can do all things because of Christ who strengthens me.

—Philippians 4:11–13

But, godliness with contentment is great gain. For we brought nothing into this world, and it is certain that we can carry nothing out. If we have food and clothing, we shall be content with these things. But those who desire to be rich fall into temptation and a snare and into many foolish and harmful lusts, which drown men in ruin and destruction. For the love of money is the root of all evil. While coveting after money, some have strayed from the faith and pierced themselves through with many sorrows.

—1 Timothy 6:6–10

Command those who are rich in this world that they not be conceited, nor trust in uncertain riches, but in the living God, who richly gives us all things to enjoy. Command that they do good, that they be rich in good works, generous, willing to share.

—1 Timothy 6:17–18

CALLED TO HAVE CHARACTER

Now, Israel, what does the Lord your God require of you, but to fear the Lord your God, to walk in all His ways, to love Him, and to serve the Lord your God with all your heart and all your soul?

—Deuteronomy 10:12

You must follow after the Lord your God, fear Him, and keep His commandments, obey His voice, and you must serve Him, and cling to Him.

—Deuteronomy 13:4

Blessed is the man who walks not in the counsel of the ungodly, nor stands in the path of sinners, nor sits in the seat of scoffers; but his delight is in the law of the LORD, and in His law he meditates day and night. He will be like a tree planted by the rivers of water, that brings forth its fruit in its season. Its leaf will not wither; and whatever he does will prosper.

—PSALM 1:1–3

LORD, who will abide in Your tabernacle? Who will dwell in Your holy hill? He who walks uprightly, and does righteousness, and speaks truth in his own heart. He who does not slander with the tongue, nor does evil to his neighbor, nor bears a reproach against a person close by. In whose eyes a vile person is despised, but he honors those who fear the LORD, he swears to avoid evil and does not change. He who does not put his money out to usury, nor take a bribe against the innocent. He who does these things will never be moved.

—PSALM 15:1-5

Who may ascend the hill of the LORD? Who may stand in His holy place? He who has clean hands, and a pure heart; who has not lifted up his soul unto vanity, nor sworn deceitfully.

—PSALM 24:3–4

Blessed is everyone who fears the LORD, who walks in His ways. For you shall eat the fruit of the labor of your hands; you will be happy, and it shall be well with you.

—PSALM 128:1–2

He who walks uprightly walks surely, but he who perverts his ways will be known.

—PROVERBS 10:9

The wisdom of the prudent is to understand his way, but the folly of fools is deceit.

—PROVERBS 14:8

"For My thoughts are not your thoughts, nor are your ways My ways," says the LORD.... "For you shall go out with joy, and be led forth with peace. The mountains and the hills shall break forth before you into singing, and all the trees of the field shall clap their hands."

—ISAIAH 55:8, 12

Do not be conformed to this world, but be transformed by the renewing of your mind, that you may prove what is the good and acceptable and perfect will of God.

—ROMANS 12:2

For I say, through the grace given to me, to everyone among you, not to think of himself more highly than he ought to think, but to think with sound judgment, according to the measure of faith God has distributed to every man.

—ROMANS 12:3

See then that you walk carefully, not as fools, but as wise men, making the most of the time because the days are evil. Therefore do not be unwise, but understand what the will of the Lord is.

—EPHESIANS 5:15–17

Do all things without murmuring and disputing, that you may be blameless and harmless, sons of God, without fault, in the midst of a crooked and perverse generation, in which you shine as lights in the world.

—PHILIPPIANS 2:14–15

Take heed to yourself and to the doctrine. Continue in them, for in doing this you will save both yourself and those who hear you.

—1 TIMOTHY 4:16

But you, O man of God, escape these things, and follow after righteousness, godliness, faith, love, patience, and gentleness. Fight the good fight of faith. Lay hold on eternal life, to which you are called and have professed a good profession before many witnesses.

—1 TIMOTHY 6:11–12

Obey your leaders and submit to them, for they watch over your souls as those who must give an account. Let them do this with joy and not complaining, for that would not be profitable to you.

—Hebrews 13:17

Who is wise and understanding among you? Let him show his works by his good life in the meekness of wisdom.

—James 3:13

Be sober and watchful, because your adversary the devil walks around as a roaring lion, seeking whom he may devour.

—1 Peter 5:8

Called to Live With Integrity

Lord, who will abide in Your tabernacle? Who will dwell in Your holy hill? He who walks uprightly, and does righteousness, and speaks truth in his own heart.

—Psalm 15:1–2

You have examined my heart; You have visited me in the night; You have tried me, and found nothing; I have purposed that my mouth will not transgress.

—Psalm 17:3

For all His judgments were before me, and I did not put away His statutes from me. I was also upright before Him, and I kept myself from my iniquity.

—Psalm 18:22–23

I will set no wicked thing before my eyes. I hate the work of those who turn aside; it shall not have part of me. A perverted heart shall be far from me; I will not know anything wicked.

—Psalm 101:3–4

He lays up sound wisdom for the righteous; He is a shield to those who walk uprightly. He keeps the paths of justice, and preserves the ways of His saints. Then you will understand righteousness and judgment and equity, and every good path.

—Proverbs 2:7–9

The integrity of the upright will guide them, but the perverseness of transgressors will destroy them.

—Proverbs 11:3

Lying lips are an abomination to the Lord, but those who deal truly are His delight.

—Proverbs 12:22

The wisdom of the prudent is to understand his way, but the folly of fools is deceit. Fools make a mock at sin, but among the righteous there is favor.

—Proverbs 14:8–9

For to the person who is pleasing before Him, God gives wisdom, knowledge, and joy, but to the one who sins, He gives the task to gather and collect in order to give to the other person who is pleasing before God. Also this is vanity and chasing the wind.

—Ecclesiastes 2:26

In this do I always strive to have a clear conscience toward God and toward men.

—Acts 24:16

So it is necessary to be in subjection, not only because of wrath, but also for the sake of conscience.

—Romans 13:5

One man judges one day above another; another judges every day alike. Let each one be fully persuaded in his own mind.

—Romans 14:5

But we have renounced the secret things of shame, not walking in craftiness nor handling the word of God deceitfully, but by expressing the truth and commending ourselves to every man's conscience in the sight of God.

—2 Corinthians 4:2

Dearly beloved, I implore you as aliens and refugees, abstain from fleshly lusts, which wage war against the soul.

—1 Peter 2:11

But sanctify the Lord God in your hearts. Always be ready to give an answer to every man who asks you for a reason for the hope that is in you, with gentleness and fear. Have a good conscience so that evildoers who speak evil of you and falsely accuse your good conduct in Christ may be ashamed.

—1 Peter 3:15–16

Called to Humility

Surely, God will not cast away a perfect man, nor will He strengthen the evildoers, until He fills your mouth with laughing, and your lips with rejoicing.

—Job 8:20–21

I cried to the Lord with my voice, and He answered me from His holy hill. I lay down and slept; I awoke, for the Lord sustained me.

—Psalm 3:4–5

The desire of the humble You have heard, O Lord; You make their heart attentive.

—Psalm 10:17

It is God who clothes me with strength, and gives my way integrity.

—Psalm 18:32

The meek will He guide in judgment; and the meek He will teach His way.

—Psalm 25:9

In the fear of the Lord is strong confidence, and His children will have a place of refuge. The fear of the Lord is a fountain of life, to depart from the snares of death.

—Proverbs 14:26–27

By humility and the fear of the Lord are riches, and honor, and life.

—Proverbs 22:4

The lofty looks of man shall be humbled, and the haughtiness of men shall be bowed down, and the Lord alone shall be exalted in that day.

—Isaiah 2:11

Let the wicked forsake his way, and the unrighteous man his thoughts. And let him return to the Lord, and He will have mercy upon him, and to our God, for He will abundantly pardon.

—Isaiah 55:7

Take My yoke upon you, and learn from Me. For I am meek and lowly in heart, and you will find rest for your souls.

—Matthew 11:29

Truly I say to you, unless you are converted and become like little children, you will not enter the kingdom of heaven. Therefore whoever humbles himself like this little child is greatest in the kingdom of heaven.

—Matthew 18:3–4

For he who exalts himself will be humbled, and he who humbles himself will be exalted.

—Matthew 23:12

I tell you, this man went down to his house justified rather than the other. For everyone who exalts himself will be humbled, and he who humbles himself will be exalted.

—Luke 18:14

But you are not so. Instead, let him who is greatest among you be as the younger, and he who rules as he who serves. For who is greater: he who sits at the table, or he who serves? Is it not he who sits at the table? But I am among you as He who serves.

—LUKE 22:26–27

He must increase, but I must decrease.

—JOHN 3:30

Be of the same mind toward one another. Do not be haughty, but associate with the lowly. Do not pretend to be wiser than you are.

—ROMANS 12:16

Let no one deceive himself. If anyone among you seems to be wise in this world, let him become a fool that he may be wise. For the wisdom of this world is foolishness with God. For it is written, "He catches the wise in their own craftiness."

—1 CORINTHIANS 3:18–19

With all humility, meekness, and patience, bearing with one another in love.

—EPHESIANS 4:2

Let nothing be done out of strife or conceit, but in humility let each esteem the other better than himself. Let each of you look not only to your own interests, but also to the interests of others.

—PHILIPPIANS 2:3–4

So embrace, as the elect of God, holy and beloved, a spirit of mercy, kindness, humbleness of mind, meekness, and longsuffering.

—Colossians 3:12

One who cleanses himself from these things will be a vessel for honor, sanctified, fit for the master's use, and prepared for every good work.

—2 Timothy 2:21

Let the brother of low degree rejoice in that he is exalted.

—James 1:9

For where there is envying and strife, there is confusion and every evil work. But the wisdom that is from above is first pure, then peaceable, gentle, open to reason, full of mercy and good fruits, without partiality, and without hypocrisy.

—James 3:16–17

But He gives more grace. For this reason it says, "God resists the proud, but gives grace to the humble."

—James 4:6

Do not let your adorning be the outward adorning of braiding the hair, wearing gold, or putting on fine clothing.

—1 Peter 3:3

Likewise you younger ones, submit yourselves to the elders. Yes, all of you be submissive one to another and clothe yourselves with humility, because "God resists the proud, and gives grace to the humble." Humble yourselves under the mighty hand of God, that He may exalt you in due time.

—1 Peter 5:5–6

CALLED TO HAVE COMPASSION

But I say to you, love your enemies, bless those who curse you, do good to those who hate you, and pray for those who spitefully use you and persecute you, that you may be sons of your Father who is in heaven. For He makes His sun rise on the evil and on the good and sends rain on the just and on the unjust.

—Matthew 5:44–45

But love your enemies, and do good, and lend, hoping for nothing in return. Then your reward will be great, and you will be the sons of the Highest. For He is kind to the unthankful and the evil.

—Luke 6:35

Brothers, if a man is caught in any transgression, you who are spiritual should restore such a one in the spirit of meekness, watching yourselves, lest you also be tempted. Bear one another's burdens, and so fulfill the law of Christ. For if someone thinks himself to be something when he is nothing, he deceives himself.

—GALATIANS 6:1–3

And be kind one to another, tender-hearted, forgiving one another, just as God in Christ also forgave you.

—EPHESIANS 4:32

So embrace, as the elect of God, holy and beloved, a spirit of mercy, kindness, humbleness of mind, meekness, and long-suffering. Bear with one another and forgive one another. If anyone has a quarrel against anyone, even as Christ forgave you, so you must do.

—COLOSSIANS 3:12–13

Finally, be all of one mind, be loving toward one another, be gracious, and be kind. Do not repay evil for evil, or curse for curse, but on the contrary, bless, knowing that to this you are called, so that you may receive a blessing.

—1 PETER 3:8–9

By this we know the love of God: that He laid down His life for us, and we ought to lay down our lives for the brothers. Whoever has the world's goods and sees his brother in need, but closes his heart of compassion from him, how can the love of God remain in him? My little children, let us love not in word and speech, but in action and truth.

—1 JOHN 3:16–18

Chapter 4

HOPE FOR RELATIONSHIPS

LOVING OTHERS

You shall not take vengeance, nor bear any grudge against the children of your people, but you shall love your neighbor as yourself: for I am the LORD.

—LEVITICUS 19:18

My friends scorn me; my eyes pour out tears unto God. Oh, that one might plead for a man with God, as a man pleads for his neighbor!

—JOB 16:20–21

Like a father shows compassion to his children, so the LORD gives compassion to those who fear Him.

—PSALM 103:13

Hatred stirs up strife, but love covers all sins.

—PROVERBS 10:12

A soft answer turns away wrath, but grievous words stir up anger. The tongue of the wise uses knowledge aright, but the mouth of fools pours out foolishness.

—PROVERBS 15:1–2

The heart of the wise teaches his mouth, and adds learning to his lips. Pleasant words are as a honeycomb, sweet to the soul, and health to the bones.

—PROVERBS 16:23–24

He who covers a transgression seeks love, but he who repeats a matter separates friends.

—PROVERBS 17:9

A friend loves at all times, and a brother is born for adversity.

—PROVERBS 17:17

A man who has friends must show himself friendly, and there is a friend who sticks closer than a brother.

—PROVERBS 18:24

Faithful are the wounds of a friend, but the kisses of an enemy are deceitful.

—PROVERBS 27:6

Two are better than one because there is a good reward for their labor together. For if they fall, then one will help up his companion. But how tragic to the one who falls, and there is no one else to help him up.

—ECCLESIASTES 4:9–10

But I say to you, do not resist an evil person. But whoever strikes you on your right cheek, turn to him the other as well. And if anyone sues you in a court of law and takes away your tunic, let him have your cloak also. And whoever compels you to go a mile, go with him two. Give to him who asks you, and from him who would borrow from you do not turn away.

—Matthew 5:39–42

You have heard that it was said, "You shall love your neighbor and hate your enemy." But I say to you, love your enemies, bless those who curse you, do good to those who hate you, and pray for those who spitefully use you and per-secute you, That you may be sons of your Father who is in heaven. For He makes His sun rise on the evil and on the good and sends rain on the just and on the unjust. For if you love those who love you, what reward do you have? Do not even the tax collectors do the same? And if you greet your brothers only, what are you doing more than others? Do not even the tax collectors do so?

—Matthew 5:43–47

And when you stand praying, forgive if you have anything against anyone, so that your Father who is in heaven may also forgive you your sins.

—Mark 11:25

But I say to you who hear, love your enemies, do good to those who hate you, bless those who curse you, and pray for those who spitefully use you.... Give to everyone who asks of you. And of him who takes away your goods, do not ask for them back. Do unto others as you would have others do unto you.

—Luke 6:27–28, 30–31

But love your enemies, and do good, and lend, hoping for nothing in return. Then your reward will be great, and you will be the sons of the Highest. For He is kind to the unthankful and the evil. Be therefore merciful, even as your Father is merciful.

—Luke 6:35–36

Now, a lawyer stood up and tested Him, saying, "Teacher, what must I do to inherit eternal life?" He said to him, "What is written in the law? How do you read?" He answered, "'You shall love the Lord your God with all your heart, and with all your soul, and with all your strength, and with all your mind' and 'your neighbor as yourself.'" He said to him, "You have answered correctly. Do this, and you will live."

—Luke 10:25–28

Beloved, do not avenge yourselves, but rather give place to God's wrath, for it is written: "Vengeance is Mine. I will repay," says the Lord. Therefore "If your enemy is hungry, feed him; if he is thirsty, give him a drink, for in doing so you will heap coals of fire on his head." Do not be overcome by evil, but overcome evil with good.

—Romans 12:19–21

Therefore let us no longer pass judgment on one another, but rather determine this, not to put a stumbling block or an obstacle in a brother's way.

—Romans 14:13

I thank my God always on your behalf for the grace of God which has been given to you through Jesus Christ. By Him you are enriched in everything, in all speech and in all knowledge.

—1 Corinthians 1:4–5

He will strengthen you to the end, so that you may be blameless on the day of our Lord Jesus Christ. God is faithful, and by Him you were called to the fellowship of His Son, Jesus Christ our Lord.

—1 Corinthians 1:8–9

Finally, brothers, farewell. Be perfect, be of good comfort, be of one mind, and live in peace, and the God of love and peace will be with you.

—2 Corinthians 13:11

Let him who is taught in the word share all good things with him who teaches.

—GALATIANS 6:6

With all humility, meekness, and patience, bearing with one another in love, be eager to keep the unity of the Spirit in the bond of peace.

—EPHESIANS 4:2–3

So embrace, as the elect of God, holy and beloved, a spirit of mercy, kindness, humbleness of mind, meekness, and long-suffering. Bear with one another and forgive one another. If anyone has a quarrel against anyone, even as Christ forgave you, so you must do. And above all these things, embrace love, which is the bond of perfection.

—COLOSSIANS 3:12–14

As concerning brotherly love, you do not need me to write to you. For you yourselves are taught by God to love one another. And indeed, you do have love for all the brothers who are in all Macedonia. But we urge you, brothers, that you increase more and more.

—1 THESSALONIANS 4:9–10

See that no one renders evil for evil to anyone. But always seek to do good to one another and to all.

—1 THESSALONIANS 5:15

Above all things, have unfailing love for one another, because love covers a multitude of sins. Show hospitality to one another without complaining. As every one has received a gift, even so serve one another with it, as good stewards of the manifold grace of God.

—1 Peter 4:8–10

FORGIVING OTHERS

And forgive us our debts, as we forgive our debtors....For if you forgive men for their sins, your heavenly Father will also forgive you. But if you do not forgive men for their sins, neither will your Father forgive your sins.

—Matthew 6:12, 14–15

Take heed to yourselves. If your brother sins against you, rebuke him. And if he repents, forgive him. If he sins against you seven times in a day, and seven times in a day turns to you, saying, "I repent," you must forgive him.

—Luke 17:3–4

Whomever you forgive anything, I also forgive. For if I forgave someone anything, for your sakes I forgave it in Christ.

—2 Corinthians 2:10

And do not grieve the Holy Spirit of God, in whom you are sealed for the day of redemption....And be kind one to another, tender-hearted, forgiving one another, just as God in Christ also forgave you.

—EPHESIANS 4:30, 32

Whoever says he is in the light but hates his brother is in darkness even until now. Whoever loves his brother lives in the light, and in him there is no cause for stumbling.

—1 JOHN 2:9–10

SERVING GOD BY SERVING OTHERS

And whoever receives one such little child in My name receives Me.

—MATTHEW 18:5

And whoever would be first among you, let him be your slave, even as the Son of Man did not come to be served, but to serve and to give His life as a ransom for many.

—MATTHEW 20:27–28

He who is greatest among you shall be your servant.

—MATTHEW 23:11

Does he thank the servant because he did what was commanded? I think not. So you also, when you have done everything commanded you, say, "We are unprofitable servants. We have done our duty."

—LUKE 17:9–10

If anyone serves Me, he must follow Me. Where I am, there will My servant be also. If anyone serves Me, the Father will honor him.

—John 12:26

Be devoted to one another with brotherly love; prefer one another in honor, do not be lazy in diligence, be fervent in spirit, serve the Lord.

—Romans 12:10–11

You, brothers, have been called to liberty. Only do not use liberty to give an opportunity to the flesh, but by love, serve one another.

—Galatians 5:13

Religion that is pure and undefiled before God, the Father, is this: to visit the fatherless and widows in their affliction and to keep oneself unstained by the world.

—James 1:27

If a brother or sister is naked and lacking daily food, and one of you says to them, "Depart in peace, be warmed and filled," and yet you give them nothing that the body needs, what does it profit?

—James 2:15–16

"The joy and peace of believers arise chiefly from their hopes. What is laid out upon them is but little, compared with what is laid up for them; therefore the more hope they have, the more joy and peace they have.... Christians should desire and labour after an abundance of hope."

MATTHEW HENRY

By this we know the love of God: that He laid down His life for us, and we ought to lay down our lives for the brothers. Whoever has the world's goods and sees his brother in need, but closes his heart of compassion from him, how can the love of God remain in him?

—1 John 3:16–17

HONORING ONE ANOTHER

Behold, how good and how pleasant it is for brothers to dwell together in unity!

—Psalm 133:1

A talebearer reveals secrets, but he who is of a faithful spirit conceals the matter.

—Proverbs 11:13

He who loves pureness of heart, for the grace of his lips the king will be his friend.

—Proverbs 22:11

For whoever does the will of My Father who is in heaven is My brother, and sister, and mother.

—Matthew 12:50

Give, and it will be given to you: Good measure, pressed down, shaken together, and running over, will men give unto you. For with the measure you use, it will be measured unto you.

—Luke 6:38

This is My commandment: that you love one another, as I have loved you. Greater love has no man than this: that a man lay down his life for his friends.

—John 15:12–13

You are My friends if you do whatever I command you. I no longer call you servants, for a servant does not know what his master does. But I have called you friends, for everything that I have heard from My Father have I made known to you.

—John 15:14–15

For just as we have many parts in one body, and not all parts have the same function, so we, being many, are one body in Christ, and all are parts of one another. We have diverse gifts according to the grace that is given to us: if prophecy, according to the proportion of faith.

—Romans 12:4–6

Rejoice with those who rejoice, and weep with those who weep. Be of the same mind toward one another. Do not be haughty, but associate with the lowly. Do not pretend to be wiser than you are.

—Romans 12:15–16

Beloved, do not avenge yourselves, but rather give place to God's wrath, for it is written: "Vengeance is Mine. I will repay," says the Lord. Therefore "If your enemy is hungry, feed him; if he is thirsty, give him a drink, for in doing so you will heap coals of fire on his head." Do not be overcome by evil, but overcome evil with good.

—ROMANS 12:19–21

Love suffers long and is kind; love envies not; love flaunts not itself and is not puffed up, does not behave itself improperly, seeks not its own, is not easily provoked, thinks no evil; rejoices not in iniquity, but rejoices in the truth; bears all things, believes all things, hopes all things, and endures all things. Love never fails. But if there are prophecies, they shall fail; if there are tongues, they shall cease; and if there is knowledge, it shall vanish.

—1 CORINTHIANS 13:4–8

You are all sons of God by faith in Christ Jesus. For as many of you as have been baptized into Christ have put on Christ. There is neither Jew nor Greek, there is neither slave nor free, and there is neither male nor female, for you are all one in Christ Jesus. If you are Christ's, then you are Abraham's seed, and heirs according to the promise.

—GALATIANS 3:26–29

Likewise, older women should be reverent in behavior, and not be false accusers, not be enslaved to much wine, but teachers of good things, that they may teach the young women to love their husbands, to love their children.

—TITUS 2:3–4

And let us consider how to spur one another to love and to good works. Let us not forsake the assembling of ourselves together, as is the manner of some, but let us exhort one another, especially as you see the Day approaching.

—HEBREWS 10:24–25

Let brotherly love continue. Do not forget to entertain strangers, for thereby some have entertained angels unknowingly.

—HEBREWS 13:1–2

Above all things, have unfailing love for one another, because love covers a multitude of sins. Show hospitality to one another without complaining. As every one has received a gift, even so serve one another with it, as good stewards of the manifold grace of God.

—1 PETER 4:8–10

We declare to you that which we have seen and heard, that you also may have fellowship with us. And our fellowship is with the Father and with His Son Jesus Christ.

—1 JOHN 1:3

But if we walk in the light as He is in the light, we have fellowship one with another, and the blood of Jesus Christ His Son cleanses us from all sin.

—1 John 1:7

Showing Kindness to One Another

A despairing man should be shown kindness from his friend, or he forsakes the fear of the Almighty.

—Job 6:14

Defend the poor and fatherless, vindicate the afflicted and needy. Grant escape to the abused and the destitute, pluck them out of the hand of the false.

—Psalm 82:3–4

Ointment and perfume rejoice the heart, so does the sweetness of a man's friend by hearty counsel.

—Proverbs 27:9

He who gives to the poor will not lack, but he who hides his eyes will have many a curse.

—Proverbs 28:27

She stretches out her hand to the poor; yes, she reaches forth her hands to the needy.

—Proverbs 31:20

Therefore consider the goodness and severity of God—severity toward those who fell, but goodness toward you, if you continue in His goodness. Otherwise, you also will be cut off.

—ROMANS 11:22

We who are strong ought to bear the weaknesses of the weak and not please ourselves. Let each of us please his neighbor for his good, leading to edification.

—ROMANS 15:1–2

Likewise, older women should be reverent in behavior, and not be false accusers, not be enslaved to much wine, but teachers of good things, that they may teach the young women to love their husbands, to love their children.

—TITUS 2:4–5

For this reason, make every effort to add virtue to your faith; and to your virtue, knowledge; and to your knowledge, self-control; and to your self-control, patient endurance; and to your patient endurance, godliness; and to your godliness, brotherly kindness; and to your brotherly kindness, love. For if these things reside in you and abound, they ensure that you will neither be useless nor unfruitful in the knowledge of our Lord Jesus Christ.

—2 PETER 1:5–8

GIVING TO ONE ANOTHER

By all means give to him, and may your heart not be grieved when you give to him. For the LORD your God will bless you in all your undertakings and in all that you put your hand to do.

—DEUTERONOMY 15:10

The wicked borrows and does not repay, but the righteous is gracious and gives. For those who are blessed of Him will inherit the earth, but those who are cursed of Him will be cut off.

—PSALM 37:21–22

A good man shows generous favor, and lends; he will guide his affairs with justice.

—PSALM 112:5

The generous soul will be made rich, and he who waters will be watered also himself.

—PROVERBS 11:25

He who has pity on the poor lends to the LORD, and He will repay what he has given.

—PROVERBS 19:17

Give to him who asks you, and from him who would borrow from you do not turn away.

—Matthew 5:42

And whoever gives even a cup of cold water to one of these little ones in the name of a disciple, truly I tell you, he shall in no way lose his reward.

—Matthew 10:42

Come to Me, all you who labor and are heavily burdened, and I will give you rest. Take My yoke upon you, and learn from Me. For I am meek and lowly in heart, and you will find rest for your souls. For My yoke is easy, and My burden is light.

—Matthew 11:28–30

For I was hungry and you gave Me food, I was thirsty and you gave Me drink, I was a stranger and you took Me in. I was naked and you clothed Me, I was sick and you visited Me, I was in prison, and you came to Me.

—Matthew 25:35–36

On that day you will ask Me nothing. Truly, truly I say to you, whatever you ask the Father in My name, He will give it to you. Until now you have asked nothing in My name. Ask, and you will receive, that your joy may be full.

—John 16:23–24

Contribute to the needs of the saints, practice hospitality.

—Romans 12:13

Render to all what is due them: taxes to whom taxes are due, respect to whom respect is due, fear to whom fear is due, and honor to whom honor is due. Owe no one anything, except to love one another, for he who loves another has fulfilled the law.

—Romans 13:7–8

But this I say: He who sows sparingly will also reap sparingly, and he who sows bountifully will also reap bountifully. Let every man give according to the purposes in his heart, not grudgingly or out of necessity, for God loves a cheerful giver.

—2 Corinthians 9:6–7

But do not forget to do good and to share. For with such sacrifices God is well pleased.

—Hebrews 13:16

Encouraging One Another

As for me, I will see Your face in righteousness; I will be satisfied when I awake with Your likeness.

—Psalm 17:15

You are my hiding place; You will preserve me from trouble; You will surround me with shouts of deliverance.

—Psalm 32:7

The mouth of the righteous utters wisdom, and their tongue speaks justice.

—Psalm 37:30

For the Lord God is a sun and shield; the Lord will give favor and glory, for no good thing will He withhold from the one who walks uprightly.

—Psalm 84:11

Blessed are the people who know the joyful shout. They walk, O Lord, in the light of Your presence. In Your name they rejoice all the day, and in Your righteousness they shall be exalted. For You are the beauty of their strength; by Your favor our horn is exalted.

—Psalm 89:15–17

Though I walk in the midst of trouble, You will preserve me; You stretch forth Your hand against the wrath of my enemies, and Your right hand saves me.

—Psalm 138:7

When wisdom enters your heart and knowledge is pleasant to your soul, discretion will preserve you, understanding will keep you, to deliver you from the way of the evil man, from the man who speaks perverse things.

—Proverbs 2:10–12

There is one who speaks like the piercings of a sword, but the tongue of the wise is health.

—Proverbs 12:18

Heaviness in the heart of man makes it droop, but a good word makes it glad.

—Proverbs 12:25

A man has joy by the answer of his mouth, and a word spoken in due season, how good is it!

—Proverbs 15:23

When a man's ways please the Lord, He makes even his enemies to be at peace with him.

—Proverbs 16:7

Hear counsel and receive instruction, that you may be wise in your latter days.

—Proverbs 19:20

Have you not known? Have you not heard, that the everlasting God, the Lord, the Creator of the ends of the earth, does not faint, nor is He weary? His understanding is inscrutable. He gives power to the faint, and to those who have no might He increases strength. Even the youths shall faint and be weary, and the young men shall utterly fall. But those who wait upon the LORD shall renew their strength. They shall mount up with wings as eagles. They shall run, and not be weary. And they shall walk, and not faint.

—ISAIAH 40:28–31

"For My thoughts are not your thoughts, nor are your ways My ways," says the LORD. "For as the heavens are higher than the earth, so are My ways higher than your ways, and My thoughts than your thoughts."

—ISAIAH 55:8–9

Do not be afraid, little flock, for it is your Father's good pleasure to give you the kingdom.

—LUKE 12:32

Who shall separate us from the love of Christ? Shall tribulation, or distress, or persecution, or famine, or nakedness, or peril, or sword?

—ROMANS 8:35

For whatever was previously written was written for our instruction, so that through perseverance and encouragement of the Scriptures we might have hope. Now may the God of perseverance and encouragement grant you to live in harmony with one another in accordance with Christ Jesus, so that together you may with one voice glorify the

God and Father of our Lord Jesus Christ. Therefore welcome one another, just as Christ also welcomed us, for the glory of God.

—Romans 15:4–7

For this reason we do not lose heart: Even though our outward man is perishing, yet our inward man is being renewed day by day. Our light affliction, which lasts but for a moment, works for us a far more exceeding and eternal weight of glory, while we do not look at the things which are seen, but at the things which are not seen. For the things which are seen are temporal, but the things which are not seen are eternal.

—2 Corinthians 4:16–18

Therefore be imitators of God as beloved children. Walk in love, as Christ loved us and gave Himself for us as a fragrant offering and a sacrifice to God.

—Ephesians 5:1–2

If there is any encouragement in Christ, if any comfort of love, if any fellowship of the Spirit, if any compassion and mercy, then fulfill my joy and be like-minded, having the same love, being in unity with one mind.

—Philippians 2:1–2

I can do all things because of Christ who strengthens me.

—Philippians 4:13

If you then were raised with Christ, desire those things which are above, where Christ sits at the right hand of God. Set your affection on things above, not on things on earth.

—COLOSSIANS 3:1–2

And whatever you do, do it heartily, as to the Lord, and not for people.

—COLOSSIANS 3:23

As you know, we exhorted, comforted, and commanded every one of you, as a father does his own children, that you would walk in a manner worthy of God, who has called you to His kingdom and glory.

—1 THESSALONIANS 2:11–12

Then we who are alive and remain shall be caught up together with them in the clouds to meet the Lord in the air. And so we shall be forever with the Lord. Therefore comfort one another with these words.

—1 THESSALONIANS 4:17–18

So comfort yourselves together, and edify one another, just as you are doing.

—1 THESSALONIANS 5:11

Now may our Lord Jesus Christ Himself, and God our Father, who has loved us and has given us eternal consolation and good hope through grace, comfort your hearts and establish you in every good word and work.

—2 Thessalonians 2:16–17

But exhort one another daily, while it is called "Today," lest any of you be hardened through the deceitfulness of sin.

—Hebrews 3:13

Let us not forsake the assembling of ourselves together, as is the manner of some, but let us exhort one another, especially as you see the Day approaching.

—Hebrews 10:25

Therefore, my beloved brothers, let every man be swift to hear, slow to speak, and slow to anger.

—James 1:19

Blessed be the God and Father of our Lord Jesus Christ, who according to His abundant mercy has given us a new birth into a living hope through the resurrection of Jesus Christ from the dead, to an incorruptible and undefiled inheritance that does not fade away, kept in heaven for you.

—1 Peter 1:3–4

But you are a chosen people, a royal priesthood, a holy nation, a people for God's own possession, so that you may declare the goodness of Him who has called you out of darkness into His marvelous light.

—1 PETER 2:9

Show hospitality to one another without complaining.

—1 PETER 4:9

Beloved, now are we sons of God, and it has not yet been revealed what we shall be. But we know that when He appears, we shall be like Him, for we shall see Him as He is.

—1 JOHN 3:2

Blessed are those who do His commandments, that they may have the right to the tree of life, and may enter through the gates into the city.

—REVELATION 22:14

Chapter 5

THE ATTRIBUTES OF GOD

GOD'S FAITHFULNESS

Remember, I am with you, and I will protect you wherever you go, and I will bring you back to this land. For I will not leave you until I have done what I promised you.

—GENESIS 28:15

Know therefore that the LORD your God, He is God, the faithful God, who keeps covenant and mercy with them who love Him and keep His commandments to a thousand generations.

—DEUTERONOMY 7:9

For all His ways are just. He is a God of faithfulness and without injustice. Righteous and upright is He.

—DEUTERONOMY 32:4

The LORD requites to every man his right conduct and loyalty. So the LORD gave you into my hand today, but I am not willing to stretch my hand against the LORD's anointed.

—1 SAMUEL 26:23

All the paths of the LORD are lovingkindness and truth, for those who keep His covenant and His testimonies.

—PSALM 25:10

Oh, love the LORD, all you His saints, for the LORD preserves the faithful, but amply repays the one who acts in pride. Be strong, and He will strengthen your heart, all you who wait for the LORD.

—PSALM 31:23–24

Your mercy, O LORD, is in the heavens, and Your faithfulness reaches to the clouds.

—PSALM 36:5

Have mercy on me, O Lord, for to You I cry all day long. Gladden the soul of Your servant, for to You, O Lord, I lift my soul.

—PSALM 86:3–4

I will sing of the mercies of the Lord forever; with my mouth I will make known Your faithfulness to all generations. For I have said, "Mercy shall be built up forever; Your faithfulness shall be established in the heavens."

—PSALM 89:1–2

He shall cover you with his feathers, and under His wings you shall find protection; His faithfulness shall be your shield and wall.

—PSALM 91:4

My eyes shall be favorable to the faithful in the land, that they may live with me. He who walks in a blameless manner, he shall serve me. He who practices deceit shall not dwell within my house; he who tells lies shall not remain in my sight.

—Psalm 101:6–7

I will worship toward Your holy temple, and praise Your name for Your lovingkindness and for Your truth; for You have exalted Your word above all Your name.

—Psalm 138:2

Do not let mercy and truth forsake you; bind them around your neck, write them on the tablet of your heart. So will you find favor and good understanding in the sight of God and man.

—Proverbs 3:3–4

It is of the Lord's mercies that we are not consumed, because His compassions do not fail. They are new every morning. Great is Your faithfulness.

—Lamentations 3:22–23

His master said to him, "Well done, you good and faithful servant. You have been faithful over a few things. I will make you ruler over many things. Enter the joy of your master."

—Matthew 25:21

There are various gifts, but the same Spirit. There are differences of administrations, but the same Lord. There are various operations, but it is the same God who operates them all in all people.

—1 Corinthians 12:4–6

For as the body is one and has many parts, and all the many parts of that one body are one body, so also is Christ.

—1 Corinthians 12:12

But the fruit of the Spirit is love, joy, peace, patience, gentleness, goodness, faith, meekness, and self-control; against such there is no law.

—Galatians 5:22–23

Faithful is He who calls you, who also will do it.

—1 Thessalonians 5:24

GOD'S FORGIVENESS

The Lord is slow to anger and abounding in mercy, forgiving iniquity and transgression; but He will by no means clear the guilty, visiting the iniquity of the fathers upon the children to the third and fourth generation.

—Numbers 14:18

For Your name's sake, O Lord, pardon my iniquity, for it is great.

—Psalm 25:11

Blessed is he whose transgression is forgiven, whose sin is covered. Blessed is the man against whom the Lord does not count iniquity, and in whose spirit there is no deceit.

—Psalm 32:1–2

Rest in the Lord, and wait patiently for Him; do not fret because of those who prosper in their way, because of those who make wicked schemes. Let go of anger, and forsake wrath; do not fret—it surely leads to evil deeds.

—Psalm 37:7–8

You have forgiven the iniquity of Your people; You have covered all their sin.

—Psalm 85:2

As far as the east is from the west, so far has He removed our transgressions from us.

—Psalm 103:12

"Come now, let us reason together," says the Lord. "Though your sins be as scarlet, they shall be as white as snow. Though they be red like crimson, they shall be as wool."

—Isaiah 1:18

I will cleanse them from all their iniquity whereby they have sinned against Me. And I will pardon all their iniquities whereby they have sinned and whereby they have transgressed against Me.

—JEREMIAH 33:8

For if you forgive men for their sins, your heavenly Father will also forgive you. But if you do not forgive men for their sins, neither will your Father forgive your sins.

—MATTHEW 6:14–15

Then Peter came to Him and said, "Lord, how often shall I forgive my brother who sins against me? Up to seven times?" Jesus said to him, "I do not say to you up to seven times, but up to seventy times seven."

—MATTHEW 18:21–22

Truly I say to you, all sins will be forgiven the sons of men, and whatever blasphemies they speak.

—MARK 3:28

Blessed be the Lord God of Israel, for He has visited and redeemed His people.

—LUKE 1:68

The scribes and the Pharisees watched Him to see whether He would heal on the Sabbath, so that they might find an accusation against Him.

—Luke 6:7

Judge not, and you shall not be judged. Condemn not, and you will not be condemned. Forgive, and you shall be forgiven.

—Luke 6:37

Peter said to them, "Repent and be baptized, every one of you, in the name of Jesus Christ for the forgiveness of sins, and you shall receive the gift of the Holy Spirit. For the promise is to you, and to your children, and to all who are far away, as many as the Lord our God will call."

—Acts 2:38–39

In Him we have redemption through His blood and the forgiveness of sins according to the riches of His grace, which He lavished on us in all wisdom and insight.

—Ephesians 1:7–8

He has delivered us from the power of darkness and has transferred us into the kingdom of His dear Son, in whom we have redemption through His blood, the forgiveness of sins.

—Colossians 1:13–14

Bear with one another and forgive one another. If anyone has a quarrel against anyone, even as Christ forgave you, so you must do.

—COLOSSIANS 3:13

Then He says, "Their sins and iniquities will I remember no more." Now where there is forgiveness of these, there is no longer an offering for sin.

—HEBREWS 10:17–18

If we confess our sins, He is faithful and just to forgive us our sins and cleanse us from all unrighteousness.

—1 JOHN 1:9

GOD'S GRACE

But the salvation of the righteous is from the LORD; He is their refuge in the time of distress. The LORD will help them and deliver them; He will deliver them from the wicked, and save them, because they take refuge in Him.

—PSALM 37:39–40

We have all received from His fullness grace upon grace.

—JOHN 1:16

Therefore, since we have been justified by faith, we have peace with God through our Lord Jesus Christ, through whom we also have access by faith into this grace in which we stand, and so we rejoice in hope of the glory of God.

—Romans 5:1–2

For sin shall not have dominion over you, for you are not under the law, but under grace.

—Romans 6:14

For by grace you have been saved through faith, and this is not of yourselves. It is the gift of God, not of works, so that no one should boast.

—Ephesians 2:8–9

Let your speech always be with grace, seasoned with salt, that you may know how you should answer everyone.

—Colossians 4:6

So do not be ashamed of the testimony of our Lord, nor of me, His prisoner. But share in the sufferings of the gospel by the power of God, who has saved us, and called us with a holy calling, not by our works, but by His own purpose and grace, which was given us in Christ Jesus before the world began, but is now revealed by the appearing of our Savior, Jesus Christ, who has abolished death and has brought life and immortality to light through the gospel.

—2 Timothy 1:8–10

For we do not have a High Priest who cannot sympathize with our weaknesses, but One who was in every sense tempted like we are, yet without sin. Let us then come with confidence to the throne of grace, that we may obtain mercy and find grace to help in time of need.

—Hebrews 4:15–16

As every one has received a gift, even so serve one another with it, as good stewards of the manifold grace of God.

—1 Peter 4:10

God's Mercy

Blessed are the merciful, for they shall obtain mercy.

—Matthew 5:7

But God, being rich in mercy, because of His great love with which He loved us, even when we were dead in sins, made us alive together with Christ (by grace you have been saved).

—Ephesians 2:4–5

Let us then come with confidence to the throne of grace, that we may obtain mercy and find grace to help in time of need.

—Hebrews 4:16

For he who has shown no mercy will have judgment without mercy, for mercy triumphs over judgment.

—James 2:13

But the wisdom that is from above is first pure, then peaceable, gentle, open to reason, full of mercy and good fruits, without partiality, and without hypocrisy.

—James 3:17

GOD'S PROTECTION

But You, O Lord, are a shield for me, my glory and the one who raises up my head.

—Psalm 3:3

I will both lie down in peace and sleep; for You, Lord, make me dwell safely and securely.

—Psalm 4:8

When wisdom enters your heart and knowledge is pleasant to your soul, discretion will preserve you, understanding will keep you, to deliver you from the way of the evil man, from the man who speaks perverse things.

—Proverbs 2:10–12

I am the good shepherd. The good shepherd lays down His life for the sheep....I am the good shepherd. I know My sheep, and am known by My own.

—John 10:11, 14

Now to Him who is able to keep you from falling and to present you blameless before the presence of His glory with rejoicing.

—Jude 24

God's Blessings

Sing to the Lord, for He triumphed gloriously; the horse and his rider He has hurled into the sea.

—Exodus 15:21

O taste and see that the Lord is good; blessed is the one who seeks refuge in Him. O fear the Lord, you His saints; for the ones who fear Him will not be in need. The young lions are in want and suffer hunger, but the ones who seek the Lord will not lack any good thing.

—Psalm 34:8–10

"*Praise, like prayer, is one great means of promoting the growth of the spiritual life. It helps to remove our burdens, to excite our hope, to increase our faith.*"

CHARLES SPURGEON

For the arms of the wicked will be broken, but the LORD supports the righteous. The LORD knows the days of people of integrity, and their inheritance will be forever. They will not be ashamed in the evil time, and in the days of famine they will be satisfied.

—PSALM 37:17–19

This is the day that the LORD has made; we will rejoice and be glad in it!

—PSALM 118:24

Honor the LORD with your substance and with the first-fruits of all your increase; so your barns will be filled with plenty, and your presses will burst out with new wine.

—PROVERBS 3:9–10

The blessing of the LORD makes rich, and He adds no sorrow with it.

—PROVERBS 10:22

Commit your works to the LORD, and your thoughts will be established.

—PROVERBS 16:3

She looks well to the ways of her household, and does not eat the bread of idleness. Her children arise up, and call her blessed; her husband also, and he praises her. "Many daughters have done virtuously, but you excel them all."

—Proverbs 31:27–29

Blessed are the meek, for they shall inherit the earth. Blessed are those who hunger and thirst for righteousness, for they shall be filled. Blessed are the merciful, for they shall obtain mercy.

—Matthew 5:5–7

For there is no distinction between Jew and Greek, for the same Lord over all is generous toward all who call upon Him. For, "Every one who calls on the name of the Lord shall be saved."

—Romans 10:12–13

Blessed be the God and Father of our Lord Jesus Christ, who has blessed us with every spiritual blessing in the heavenly places in Christ, just as He chose us in Him before the foundation of the world, to be holy and blameless before Him in love.

—Ephesians 1:3–4

For we are His workmanship, created in Christ Jesus for good works, which God prepared beforehand, so that we should walk in them.

—Ephesians 2:10

For God is not unjust so as to forget your work and labor of love that you have shown for His name, in that you have ministered to the saints and continue ministering.

—HEBREWS 6:10

Every good gift and every perfect gift is from above and comes down from the Father of lights, with whom is no change or shadow of turning.

—JAMES 1:17

To an incorruptible and undefiled inheritance that does not fade away, kept in heaven for you, who are protected by the power of God through faith for a salvation ready to be revealed in the last time.

—1 PETER 1:4–5

GOD'S COMFORT

The LORD also will be a refuge for the oppressed, a refuge in times of trouble. Those who know Your name will put their trust in You, for You, LORD, have not forsaken those who seek You.

—PSALM 9:9–10

Keep me as the apple of Your eye, hide me under the shadow of Your wings.

—PSALM 17:8

Even though I walk through the valley of the shadow of death, I will fear no evil for You are with me; Your rod and Your staff they comfort me.

—Psalm 23:4

The righteous cry, and the Lord hears, and delivers them out of all their troubles. The Lord is near to the broken hearted, and saves the contrite of spirit.

—Psalm 34:17–18

You keep account of my wandering; put my tears in Your bottle; are they not in Your book?…In God I trust, I will not fear; what can a man do to me?

—Psalm 56:8, 11

Hear my cry, O God, attend to my prayer.

—Psalm 61:1

In the day when I cried You answered me, and strengthened me in my soul.

—Psalm 138:3

The Lord will fulfill His purpose for me; Your mercy, O Lord, endures forever. Do not forsake the works of Your hands.

—Psalm 138:8

You will eat and be satisfied! You will praise the name of the LORD your God who worked wonders for you. My people will be shamed no more.

—JOEL 2:26

Come to Me, all you who labor and are heavily burdened, and I will give you rest. Take My yoke upon you, and learn from Me. For I am meek and lowly in heart, and you will find rest for your souls.

—MATTHEW 11:28–29

For I am persuaded that neither death nor life, neither angels nor principalities nor powers, neither things present nor things to come, neither height nor depth, nor any other created thing, shall be able to separate us from the love of God, which is in Christ Jesus our Lord.

—ROMANS 8:38–39

What agreement has the temple of God with idols? For you are the temple of the living God. As God has said, "I will live in them, and walk in them, and I will be their God, and they shall be My people."

—2 CORINTHIANS 6:16

My brothers, count it all joy when you fall into diverse temptations, knowing that the trying of your faith develops patience. But let patience perfect its work, that you may be perfect and complete, lacking nothing.

—James 1:2–4

Therefore be patient, brothers, until the coming of the Lord. Notice how the farmer waits for the precious fruit of the earth and is patient with it until he receives the early and late rain. You also be patient. Establish your hearts, for the coming of the Lord is drawing near.

—James 5:7–8

May mercy, peace, and love be multiplied to you.

—Jude 2

God's Direction

The Lord is the portion of my inheritance and of my cup; You support my lot.

—Psalm 16:5

He who has clean hands, and a pure heart; who has not lifted up his soul unto vanity, nor sworn deceitfully. He will receive the blessing from the Lord, and righteousness from the God of his salvation.

—Psalm 24:4–5

Show me Your ways, O LORD, teach me Your paths. Lead me in Your truth and teach me, for You are my saving God, for You I wait all day long.

—PSALM 25:4–5

He who walks uprightly walks surely, but he who perverts his ways will be known.

—PROVERBS 10:9

The fruit of the righteous is a tree of life, and he who wins souls is wise.

—PROVERBS 11:30

You know the commandments, "Do not commit adultery, Do not kill, Do not steal, Do not bear false witness, Do not defraud, Honor your father and mother."

—MARK 10:19

He who is faithful in what is least is faithful also in much. And he who is dishonest in the least is dishonest also in much.

—LUKE 16:10

Be devoted to one another with brotherly love; prefer one another in honor.

—ROMANS 12:10

Repay no one evil for evil. Commend what is honest in the sight of all men. If it is possible, as much as it depends on you, live peaceably with all men.

—Romans 12:17–18

The faith that you have, have as your own conviction before God. Happy is he who does not condemn himself in what he approves.

—Romans 14:22

That you put off the former way of life in the old nature, which is corrupt according to the deceitful lusts, and be renewed in the spirit of your mind; and that you put on the new nature, which was created according to God in righteousness and true holiness.

—Ephesians 4:22–24

If there is any encouragement in Christ, if any comfort of love, if any fellowship of the Spirit, if any compassion and mercy, then fulfill my joy and be like-minded, having the same love, being in unity with one mind. Let nothing be done out of strife or conceit, but in humility let each esteem the other better than himself. Let each of you look not only to your own interests, but also to the interests of others.

—Philippians 2:1–4

Finally, brothers, whatever things are true, whatever things are honest, whatever things are just, whatever things are pure, whatever things are lovely, whatever things are of good report, if there is any virtue, and if there is any praise, think on these things.

—PHILIPPIANS 4:8

Servants, obey your masters in all things according to the flesh, serving not only when they are watching, as the servants of men, but in singleness of heart, fearing God. And whatever you do, do it heartily, as to the Lord, and not for people.

—COLOSSIANS 3:22–23

In all things presenting yourself as an example of good works: in doctrine, showing integrity, seriousness, sincerity, and sound speech that cannot be condemned, so that the one who opposes you may be ashamed, having nothing evil to say of you.

—TITUS 2:7–8

For the grace of God that brings salvation has appeared to all men, teaching us that, denying ungodliness and worldly desires, we should live soberly, righteously, and in godliness in this present world.

—TITUS 2:11–12

So speak and so do as those who will be judged by the law of liberty. For he who has shown no mercy will have judgment without mercy, for mercy triumphs over judgment.

—James 2:12–13

As obedient children do not conduct yourselves according to the former lusts in your ignorance. But as He who has called you is holy, so be holy in all your conduct.

—1 Peter 1:14–15

Live your lives honorably among the Gentiles, so that though they speak against you as evildoers, they shall see your good works and thereby glorify God in the day of visitation.

—1 Peter 2:12

Be sober and watchful, because your adversary the devil walks around as a roaring lion, seeking whom he may devour. Resist him firmly in the faith, knowing that the same afflictions are experienced by your brotherhood throughout the world.

—1 Peter 5:8–9

God's Trustworthiness

Offer sacrifices of righteousness, and trust in the Lord.

—Psalm 4:5

The law of the LORD is perfect, converting the soul. The testimony of the LORD is sure, making wise the simple. The statutes of the LORD are right, rejoicing the heart. The commandment of the LORD is pure, enlightening the eyes....More to be desired are they than gold, yes, than much fine gold; sweeter also than honey and the honeycomb.

—PSALM 19:7–8, 10

Many sorrows come to the wicked, but lovingkindness will surround the man who trusts in the LORD.

—PSALM 32:10

O taste and see that the LORD is good; blessed is the one who seeks refuge in Him.

—PSALM 34:8

Delight yourself in the LORD, and He will give you the desires of your heart. Commit your way to the LORD; trust also in Him, and He will bring it to pass.

—PSALM 37:4–5

Why are you cast down, O my soul? And why are you disquieted within me? Hope in God; for I will yet give Him thanks, the salvation of my countenance and my God.

—PSALM 43:5

O LORD of Hosts, blessed is the man who trusts in You.

—PSALM 84:12

Trust in the LORD with all your heart, and lean not on your own understanding. In all your ways acknowledge Him, and He will direct your paths.

—PROVERBS 3:5–6

He who handles a matter wisely will find good, and whoever trusts in the LORD, happy is he.

—PROVERBS 16:20

He who is of a proud heart stirs up strife, but he who puts his trust in the LORD will prosper.

—PROVERBS 28:25

When He had called the people to Him, with His disciples, He said to them, "If any man would come after Me, let him deny himself and take up his cross and follow Me. For whoever would save his life will lose it. But whoever would lose his life for My sake and the gospel's will save it."

—MARK 8:34–35

He did not waver at the promise of God through unbelief, but was strong in faith, giving glory to God, and being fully persuaded that what God had promised, He was able to perform.

—ROMANS 4:20–21

For the Scripture says, "Whoever believes in Him will not be ashamed."

—ROMANS 10:11

Cast all your care upon Him, because He cares for you.

—1 PETER 5:7

And we know that the Son of God has come and has given us understanding, so that we may know Him who is true, and we are in Him who is true—His Son Jesus Christ. He is the true God and eternal life.

—1 JOHN 5:20

Chapter 6

HOPE FOR THE BELIEVER

SALVATION

For God so loved the world that He gave His only begotten Son, that whoever believes in Him should not perish, but have eternal life. For God did not send His Son into the world to condemn the world, but that the world through Him might be saved.

—JOHN 3:16–17

He who believes in the Son has eternal life. He who does not believe the Son shall not see life, but the wrath of God remains on him.

—JOHN 3:36

My sheep hear My voice, I know them, and they follow Me. I give them eternal life. They shall never perish, nor shall anyone snatch them from My hand. My Father, who has given them to Me, is greater than all. No one is able to snatch them from My Father's hand.

—JOHN 10:27–29

For all have sinned and come short of the glory of God, being justified freely by His grace through the redemption that is in Christ Jesus.

—Romans 3:23–24

My little children, I am writing these things to you, so that you do not sin. But if anyone does sin, we have an Advocate with the Father, Jesus Christ the Righteous One. He is the atoning sacrifice for our sins, and not for ours only, but also for the sins of the whole world.

—1 John 2:1–2

Eternal Life

Surely goodness and mercy will follow me all the days of my life, and I will dwell in the house of the Lord forever.

—Psalm 23:6

And everyone who has left houses or brothers or sisters or father or mother or children or fields for My name's sake shall receive a hundred times as much and inherit eternal life. But many who are first will be last, and the last first.

—Matthew 19:29–30

For God so loved the world that He gave His only begotten Son, that whoever believes in Him should not perish, but have eternal life.

—John 3:16

But whoever drinks of the water that I shall give him will never thirst. Indeed, the water that I shall give him will become in him a well of water springing up into eternal life.

—John 4:14

Truly, truly I say to you, whoever hears My word and believes in Him who sent Me has eternal life and shall not come into condemnation, but has passed from death into life.

—John 5:24

Truly, truly I say to you, whoever believes in Me has eternal life.

—John 6:47

The thief does not come, except to steal and kill and destroy. I came that they may have life, and that they may have it more abundantly.

—John 10:10

My sheep hear My voice, I know them, and they follow Me. I give them eternal life. They shall never perish, nor shall anyone snatch them from My hand.

—John 10:27–28

Jesus said to her, "I am the resurrection and the life. He who believes in Me, though he may die, yet shall he live.

And whoever lives and believes in Me shall never die. Do you believe this?"

—JOHN 11:25–26

In My Father's house are many dwelling places. If it were not so, I would have told you. I am going to prepare a place for you. And if I go and prepare a place for you, I will come again and receive you to Myself, that where I am, you may be also.

—JOHN 14:2–3

But now, having been freed from sin and having become slaves of God, you have fruit unto holiness, and the end is eternal life. For the wages of sin is death, but the gift of God is eternal life through Jesus Christ our Lord.

—ROMANS 6:22–23

That if you confess with your mouth Jesus is Lord, and believe in your heart that God has raised Him from the dead, you will be saved.

—ROMANS 10:9

Fight the good fight of faith. Lay hold on eternal life, to which you are called and have professed a good profession before many witnesses.

—1 TIMOTHY 6:12

And this is the testimony: that God has given us eternal life, and this life is in His Son. Whoever has the Son has life, and whoever does not have the Son of God does not have life.

—1 John 5:11–12

Keep yourselves in the love of God while you are waiting for the mercy of our Lord Jesus Christ, which leads to eternal life.

—Jude 21

TEMPTATION

Watch and pray that you enter not into temptation. The spirit indeed is willing, but the flesh is weak.

—Matthew 26:41

If one part suffers, all the parts suffer with it, and if one part is honored, all the parts rejoice with it.

—1 Corinthians 12:26

Be angry but do not sin. Do not let the sun go down on your anger. Do not give place to the devil.

—Ephesians 4:26–27

Finally, my brothers, be strong in the Lord and in the power of His might. Put on the whole armor of God that you may be able to stand against the schemes of the devil. For our fight is not against flesh and blood, but against principalities, against powers, against the rulers of the darkness of this world, and against spiritual forces of evil in the heavenly places.

—Ephesians 6:10–12

Then the Lord knows how to rescue the godly from trial, and to keep the unrighteous under punishment for the Day of Judgment.

—2 Peter 2:9

Sin

God overlooked the times of ignorance, but now He commands all men everywhere to repent.

—Acts 17:30

Therefore by the works of the law no flesh will be justified in His sight, for through the law comes the knowledge of sin.

—Romans 3:20

For all have sinned and come short of the glory of God.

—Romans 3:23

Knowing this, that our old man has been crucified with Him, so that the body of sin might be destroyed, and we should no longer be slaves to sin. For the one who has died is freed from sin.

—Romans 6:6–7

Knowing that Christ, being raised from the dead, will never die again; death has no further dominion over Him. For the death He died, He died to sin once for all, but the life He lives, He lives to God. Likewise, you also consider yourselves to be dead to sin, but alive to God through Jesus Christ our Lord.

—Romans 6:9–11

There is therefore now no condemnation for those who are in Christ Jesus, who walk not according to the flesh, but according to the Spirit. For the law of the Spirit of life in Christ Jesus has set me free from the law of sin and death.

—Romans 8:1–2

Love suffers long and is kind; love envies not; love flaunts not itself and is not puffed up.

—1 Corinthians 13:4

He delivered us from so great a death and does deliver us. In Him we trust that He will still deliver us.

—2 Corinthians 1:10

Be not deceived. God is not mocked. For whatever a man sows, that will he also reap. For the one who sows to his own flesh will from the flesh reap corruption, but the one who sows to the Spirit will from the Spirit reap eternal life.

—Galatians 6:7–8

The Lord will deliver me from every evil work and will preserve me for His heavenly kingdom, to whom be glory forever and ever. Amen.

—2 Timothy 4:18

For since He Himself suffered while being tempted, He is able to help those who are being tempted.

—Hebrews 2:18

Therefore submit yourselves to God. Resist the devil, and he will flee from you.

—James 4:7

If we say that we have fellowship with Him, yet walk in darkness, we lie and do not practice the truth.

—1 John 1:6

If we say that we have no sin, we deceive ourselves, and the truth is not in us. If we confess our sins, He is faithful and just to forgive us our sins and cleanse us from all unrighteousness. If we say that we have not sinned, we make Him a liar and His word is not in us.

—1 John 1:8–10

You know that He was revealed to take away our sins, and in Him there is no sin. Whoever remains in Him does not sin. Whoever sins has not seen Him and does not know Him.

—1 John 3:5–6

REPENTANCE

I acknowledged my sin to You, and my iniquity I did not conceal. I said, "I will confess my transgressions to the Lord," and You forgave the iniquity of my sin.

—Psalm 32:5

Blessed are the peacemakers, for they shall be called the sons of God.

—Matthew 5:9

Likewise, I tell you, there will be more joy in heaven over one sinner who repents than over ninety-nine righteous men who need no repentance.

—Luke 15:7

Peter said to them, "Repent and be baptized, every one of you, in the name of Jesus Christ for the forgiveness of sins, and you shall receive the gift of the Holy Spirit."

—Acts 2:38

So why do you judge your brother? Or why do you despise your brother? For we shall all stand before the judgment seat of Christ.

—ROMANS 14:10

FORGIVENESS

Jesus answered them, "Truly, truly I say to you, whoever commits sin is a slave of sin. Now a slave does not remain in the house forever, but a son remains forever."

—JOHN 8:34–36

For you have not received the spirit of slavery again to fear. But you have received the Spirit of adoption, by whom we cry, "Abba, Father." The Spirit Himself bears witness with our spirits that we are the children of God.

—ROMANS 8:15–16

All this is from God, who has reconciled us to Himself through Jesus Christ and has given to us the ministry of reconciliation, that is, that God was in Christ reconciling the world to Himself, not counting their sins against them, and has entrusted to us the message of reconciliation.

—2 CORINTHIANS 5:18–19

In Him we have redemption through His blood and the forgiveness of sins according to the riches of His grace.

—EPHESIANS 1:7

For it pleased the Father that in Him all fullness should dwell, and to reconcile all things to Himself by Him, having made peace through the blood of His cross, by Him.

—Colossians 1:19–20

Righteousness

Trust in the Lord and do good; dwell in the land and practice faithfulness.

—Psalm 37:3

I must do the works of Him who sent Me while it is day. Night is coming when no one can work. While I am in the world, I am the light of the world.

—John 9:4–5

I have been crucified with Christ. It is no longer I who live, but Christ who lives in me. And the life I now live in the flesh, I live by faith in the Son of God, who loved me and gave Himself for me. I do not nullify the grace of God. For if righteousness comes by the law, then Christ died in vain.

—Galatians 2:20–21

That you may approve things that are excellent so that you may be pure and blameless for the day of Christ, being filled with the fruit of righteousness, which comes through Jesus Christ, for the glory and praise of God.

—Philippians 1:10–11

May the very God of peace sanctify you completely. And I pray to God that your whole spirit, soul, and body be preserved blameless unto the coming of our Lord Jesus Christ. Faithful is He who calls you, who also will do it.

—1 Thessalonians 5:23–24

SANCTIFICATION

To be carnally minded is death, but to be spiritually minded is life and peace, for the carnal mind is hostile toward God, for it is not subject to the law of God, nor indeed can it be, and those who are in the flesh cannot please God.

—Romans 8:6–8

Do you not know that the unrighteous will not inherit the kingdom of God? Do not be deceived. Neither the sexually immoral, nor idolaters, nor adulterers, nor male prostitutes, nor homosexuals, nor thieves, nor covetous, nor drunkards, nor revilers, nor extortioners will inherit the kingdom of God. Such were some of you. But you were washed, you were sanctified, and you were justified in the name of the Lord Jesus by the Spirit of our God.

—1 Corinthians 6:9–11

But we all, seeing the glory of the Lord with unveiled faces, as in a mirror, are being transformed into the same image from glory to glory by the Spirit of the Lord.

—2 Corinthians 3:18

For both He who sanctifies and those who are sanctified are all of One. For this reason He is not ashamed to call them brothers.

—Hebrews 2:11

How much more shall the blood of Christ, who through the eternal Spirit offered Himself without blemish to God, cleanse your conscience from dead works to serve the living God?

—Hebrews 9:14

Spiritual Growth

My son, keep your father's commandment, and do not forsake the instruction of your mother. Bind them continually upon your heart, and tie them around your neck. When you go, they will lead you; when you sleep, they will keep you; and when you awake, they will speak with you. For the commandment is a lamp, and the law is light; and reproofs of instruction are the way of life.

—Proverbs 6:20–23

Blessed are those who hunger and thirst for righteousness, for they shall be filled.

—Matthew 5:6

He who loves father or mother more than Me is not worthy of Me. And he who loves son or daughter more than Me is not worthy of Me. And He who does not take his cross and follow after Me is not worthy of Me. He who finds his life will lose it, and he who loses his life for My sake will find it.

—Matthew 10:37–39

Still others are seed sown on good ground, those who hear the word, and receive it, and bear fruit: thirty, sixty, or a hundred times as much.

—Mark 4:20

When He had called the people to Him, with His disciples, He said to them, "If any man would come after Me, let him deny himself and take up his cross and follow Me. For whoever would save his life will lose it. But whoever would lose his life for My sake and the gospel's will save it."

—Mark 8:34–35

Do not work for the food which perishes, but for that food which endures to eternal life, which the Son of Man will give you. For God the Father has set His seal on Him.

—John 6:27

If you know these things, blessed are you if you do them.

—John 13:17

Jesus answered him, "If a man loves Me, he will keep My word. My Father will love him, and We will come to him, and make Our home with him."

—JOHN 14:23

I am the vine, you are the branches. He who remains in Me, and I in him, bears much fruit. For without Me you can do nothing.

—JOHN 15:5

Now thanks be to God who always causes us to triumph in Christ and through us reveals the fragrance of His knowledge in every place.

—2 CORINTHIANS 2:14

That He would give you, according to the riches of His glory, power to be strengthened by His Spirit in the inner man, and that Christ may dwell in your hearts through faith; that you, being rooted and grounded in love, may be able to comprehend with all saints what is the breadth and length and depth and height, and to know the love of Christ which surpasses knowledge; that you may be filled with all the fullness of God.

—EPHESIANS 3:16–19

So we may no longer be children, tossed here and there by waves and carried about with every wind of doctrine by the trickery of men, by craftiness with deceitful scheming. But, speaking the truth in love, we may grow up in all things into Him, who is the head, Christ Himself.

—EPHESIANS 4:14–15

Therefore take up the whole armor of God that you may be able to resist in the evil day, and having done all, to stand. Stand therefore, having your waist girded with truth, having put on the breastplate of righteousness, having your feet fitted with the readiness of the gospel of peace, and above all, taking the shield of faith, with which you will be able to extinguish all the fiery arrows of the evil one. Take the helmet of salvation and the sword of the Spirit, which is the word of God.

—EPHESIANS 6:13–17

So do not be ashamed of the testimony of our Lord, nor of me, His prisoner. But share in the sufferings of the gospel by the power of God, who has saved us, and called us with a holy calling, not by our works, but by His own purpose and grace, which was given us in Christ Jesus before the world began.

—2 TIMOTHY 1:8–9

Study to show yourself approved by God, a workman who need not be ashamed, rightly dividing the word of truth.

—2 TIMOTHY 2:15

"To be assured of our salvation is no arrogant stoutness; it is our faith. It is no pride; it is devotion. It is no presumption; it is God's promise."

SAINT AUGUSTINE

The servant of the Lord must not quarrel, but must be gentle toward all people, able to teach, patient.

—2 Timothy 2:24

For whom the Lord loves He disciplines, and He scourges every son whom He receives.

—Hebrews 12:6

Be doers of the word and not hearers only, deceiving yourselves.

—James 1:22

But grow in the grace and knowledge of our Lord and Savior Jesus Christ. To Him be glory, both now and forever. Amen.

—2 Peter 3:18

Spiritual Warfare

Your right hand, O Lord, is glorious in power. Your right hand, O Lord, shatters the enemy. In the greatness of Your excellence, You overthrow those who rise up against You. You send out Your wrath;it consumes them like stubble.

—Exodus 15:6–7

The hand of our God upon all who seek Him is for good, but His power and His wrath are against all who forsake Him.

—Ezra 8:22

Surely you have spoken in my hearing, and I have heard the sound of your words saying, "I am clean, without transgression, I am innocent, nor is there iniquity in me."

—JOB 33:8–9

For You have maintained my right and my cause; You sat on the throne judging what is right. You have rebuked the nations, You have destroyed the wicked, You have wiped out their name forever and ever.

—PSALM 9:4–5

And have not delivered me up into the hand of the enemy; You have set my feet in a broad place.

—PSALM 31:8

For You have been a refuge for me, and a strong tower from the enemy.

—PSALM 61:3

For the enemy has persecuted my soul, he has crushed my life down to the ground; he has made me to dwell in darkness, as those who have been long dead. Therefore my spirit is overwhelmed within me; my heart within me is desolate.

—PSALM 143:3–4

Then you shall delight yourself in the LORD, and I will cause you to ride upon the high places of the earth, and feed you with the heritage of Jacob your father. For the mouth of the Lord has spoken it.

—Isaiah 58:14

He told them another parable, saying, "The kingdom of heaven is like a man who sowed good seed in his field. But while men slept, his enemy came and sowed weeds among the wheat and went away."

—Matthew 13:24–25

Look, I give you authority to trample on serpents and scorpions, and over all the power of the enemy. And nothing shall by any means hurt you.

—Luke 10:19

Then Saul, who also is called Paul, filled with the Holy Spirit, stared at him and said, "You son of the devil, enemy of all righteousness, full of deceit and of all fraud, will you not cease perverting the right ways of the Lord?"

—Acts 13:9–10

Therefore, my beloved brothers, be steadfast, unmovable, always abounding in the work of the Lord, knowing that your labor in the Lord is not in vain.

—1 Corinthians 15:58

Take the helmet of salvation and the sword of the Spirit, which is the word of God. Pray in the Spirit always with all kinds of prayer and supplication. To that end be alert with all perseverance and supplication for all the saints.

—Ephesians 6:17–18

Rejoice always. Pray without ceasing. In everything give thanks, for this is the will of God in Christ Jesus concerning you.

—1 Thessalonians 5:16–18

You are of God, little children, and have overcome them, because He who is in you is greater than he who is in the world.

—1 John 4:4

Seeking God

Tremble in awe, and do not sin. Commune with your own heart on your bed, and be still. Selah. Offer sacrifices of righteousness, and trust in the Lord.

—Psalm 4:4–5

Be still and know that I am God; I will be exalted among the nations, I will be exalted in the earth.

—Psalm 46:10

Therefore we are always confident, knowing that while we are at home in the body, we are absent from the Lord. For we walk by faith, not by sight.

—2 Corinthians 5:6–7

Set your affection on things above, not on things on earth. For you are dead, and your life is hidden with Christ in God.

—Colossians 3:2–3

Do not love the world or the things in the world. If anyone loves the world, the love of the Father is not in him. For all that is in the world—the lust of the flesh, the lust of the eyes, and the pride of life—is not of the Father, but is of the world. The world and its desires are passing away, but the one who does the will of God lives forever.

—1 John 2:15–17

Chapter 7

Promises for Assurance

God Will Meet Your Needs

But You, O Lord, are a shield for me, my glory and the one who raises up my head.

—Psalm 3:3

Be strong, and He will strengthen your heart, all you who wait for the Lord.

—Psalm 31:24

Let not your heart be troubled. You believe in God. Believe also in Me.

—John 14:1

Peace I leave with you. My peace I give to you. Not as the world gives do I give to you. Let not your heart be troubled, neither let it be afraid.

—John 14:27

All that the Father has are Mine. Therefore I said that He will take what is Mine and will declare it to you.

—John 16:15

Blessed be God, the Father of our Lord Jesus Christ, the Father of mercies, and the God of all comfort, who comforts us in all our tribulation, that we may be able to comfort those who are in any trouble by the comfort with which we ourselves are comforted by God.

—2 Corinthians 1:3–4

Be anxious for nothing, but in everything, by prayer and supplication with gratitude, make your requests known to God. And the peace of God, which surpasses all understanding, will protect your hearts and minds through Christ Jesus.

—Philippians 4:6–7

But the Lord is faithful, who will establish you and guard you from the evil one.

—2 Thessalonians 3:3

Therefore do not throw away your confidence, which will be greatly rewarded. For you need patience, so that after you have done the will of God, you will receive the promise.

—Hebrews 10:35–36

Knowing that the trying of your faith develops patience. But let patience perfect its work, that you may be perfect and complete, lacking nothing.

—James 1:3–4

Blessed is the man who endures temptation, for when he is tried, he will receive the crown of life, which the Lord has promised to those who love Him.

—James 1:12

Indeed we count them happy who endure. You have heard of the patience of Job and have seen the purpose of the Lord, that the Lord is very gracious and merciful.

—James 5:11

In order that the genuineness of your faith, which is more precious than gold that perishes, though it is tried by fire, may be found to result in praise, glory, and honor at the revelation of Jesus Christ.

—1 Peter 1:7

Beloved, do not be surprised at the fiery ordeal that is taking place among you to test you, as though some strange thing happened to you. But rejoice in so far as you share in Christ's sufferings, so that you may rejoice and be glad also in the revelation of His glory.

—1 Peter 4:12–13

But after you have suffered a little while, the God of all grace, who has called us to His eternal glory through Christ Jesus, will restore, support, strengthen, and establish you.

—1 Peter 5:10

DOUBT AND DISCOURAGEMENT

For who is God except the LORD? Or who is a rock besides our God? It is God who clothes me with strength, and gives my way integrity.

—PSALM 18:31–32

And let us not grow weary in doing good, for in due season we shall reap, if we do not give up.

—GALATIANS 6:9

I am confident of this very thing, that He who began a good work in you will perfect it until the day of Jesus Christ.

—PHILIPPIANS 1:6

May the very God of peace sanctify you completely. And I pray to God that your whole spirit, soul, and body be preserved blameless unto the coming of our Lord Jesus Christ.

—1 THESSALONIANS 5:23

If any of you lacks wisdom, let him ask of God, who gives to all men liberally and without criticism, and it will be given to him.

—JAMES 1:5

Fear and Disappointment

I lay down and slept; I awoke, for the Lord sustained me. I will not be afraid of multitudes of people who have set themselves against me round about.

—Psalm 3:5–6

Blessed are those who mourn, for they shall be comforted....Blessed are those who hunger and thirst for righteousness, for they shall be filled.

—Matthew 5:4, 6

Now may the God of hope fill you with all joy and peace in believing, so that you may abound in hope, through the power of the Holy Spirit.

—Romans 15:13

Watch, stand fast in the faith, be bold like men, and be strong.

—1 Corinthians 16:13

We know that if our earthly house, this tent, were to be destroyed, we have an eternal building of God in the heavens, a house not made with hands.

—2 Corinthians 5:1

GUIDANCE AND DIRECTION

Now therefore, I pray You, if I have found favor in Your sight, show me now Your way, that I may know You, and that I may find favor in Your sight. Consider too that this nation is Your people.

—Exodus 33:13

Lead me, O Lord, in Your righteousness because of my enemies. Make Your way straight before me.

—Psalm 5:8

He makes me lie down in green pastures; He leads me beside restful waters. He restores my soul; He guides me in paths of righteousness for His name's sake.

—Psalm 23:2–3

Good and upright is the Lord; therefore He will teach sinners in the way. The meek will He guide in judgment; and the meek He will teach His way.

—Psalm 25:8–9

Examine me, O Lord, and test me; try my affections and my heart. For Your lovingkindness is before my eyes, and I have walked in Your truth.

—Psalm 26:2–3

Be my strong rock, a strong fortress to save me. For You are my rock and my fortress. For Your name's sake lead me and guide me. Lead me out of the net that they have hidden for me, for You are my strength.

—Psalm 31:2–4

For this God is our God forever and ever; He will be our guide even to death.

—Psalm 48:14

You desire truth in the inward parts, and in the hidden part You make me to know wisdom.

—Psalm 51:6

Teach me Your way, O Lord, that I will walk in Your truth; bind my heart to fear Your name.

—Psalm 86:11

Cause me to hear Your lovingkindness in the morning; for in You I have my trust; cause me to know the way I should walk, for I lift up my soul unto You.

—Psalm 143:8

The preparations of the heart belong to man, but the answer of the tongue is from the Lord. All the ways of a man are clean in his own eyes, but the Lord weighs the spirit.

Commit your works to the LORD, and your thoughts will be established.

—PROVERBS 16:1–3

Therefore, everything you would like men to do to you, do also to them, for this is the Law and the Prophets.

—MATTHEW 7:12

For God, who commanded the light to shine out of darkness, has shone in our hearts to give the light of the knowledge of the glory of God in the face of Jesus Christ.

—2 CORINTHIANS 4:6

May the Lord direct your hearts to the love of God and to the steadfastness of Christ.

—2 THESSALONIANS 3:5

But the wisdom that is from above is first pure, then peaceable, gentle, open to reason, full of mercy and good fruits, without partiality, and without hypocrisy.

—JAMES 3:17

GODLY WISDOM

Who among all these does not know that the hand of the LORD has done this? In whose hand is the soul of every living thing and the breath of all mankind.

—JOB 12:9–10

From where then does wisdom come? And where is the place of understanding? It is hidden from the eyes of all living and concealed from the birds of the air. Destruction and death say, "We have heard of its fame with our ears." God understands its way, and He knows its place.

—Job 28:20–23

Look, the fear of the Lord, that is wisdom; and to depart from evil is understanding.

—Job 28:28

Let the words of my mouth and the meditation of my heart be acceptable in Your sight, O Lord, my strength, and my redeemer.

—Psalm 19:14

Make me to know Your ways, O Lord; teach me Your paths. Lead me in Your truth and teach me, for You are the God of my salvation; on You I wait all the day.

—Psalm 25:4–5

I will instruct you and teach you in the way which you will go; I will counsel you with my eye on you.

—Psalm 32:8

Your commandments have made me wiser than my enemies, for they are continually with me.

—Psalm 119:98

I will lift up my eyes to the hills, from where comes my help? My help comes from the LORD, who made heaven and earth.

—PSALM 121:1–2

My son, if you will receive my words and hide my commandments within you, so that you incline your ear to wisdom, and apply your heart to understanding; yes, if you cry out for knowledge, and lift up your voice for understanding, if you seek her as silver, and search for her as for hidden treasures, then you will understand the fear of the LORD and find the knowledge of God. For the LORD gives wisdom; out of His mouth come knowledge and understanding.

—PROVERBS 2:1–6

Trust in the LORD with all your heart, and lean not on your own understanding. In all your ways acknowledge Him, and He will direct your path. Do not be wise in your own eyes; fear the LORD and depart from evil.

—PROVERBS 3:5–7

Happy is the man who finds wisdom, and the man who gets understanding. For the proceeds of it are better than the profits of silver and the gain of fine gold.

—PROVERBS 3:13–14

Get wisdom, get understanding. Do not forget it, nor turn away from the words of my mouth. Do not forsake her, and she will preserve you; love her, and she will keep you.

Wisdom is principal; therefore get wisdom. And with all your getting get understanding.

—Proverbs 4:5–7

I have taught you in the way of wisdom; I have led you in right paths. When you walk, your steps will not be hindered, and when you run, you will not stumble.

—Proverbs 4:11–12

My son, attend to my wisdom, and bow your ear to my understanding, that you may regard discretion and that your lips may keep knowledge.

—Proverbs 5:1–2

Charm is deceitful, and beauty is vain, a woman who fears the Lord, she shall be praised.

—Proverbs 31:30

I have seen everything that is done under the sun, and indeed, all is vanity and like chasing the wind.

—Ecclesiastes 1:14

Have you not known? Have you not heard, that the everlasting God, the Lord, the Creator of the ends of the earth, does not faint, nor is He weary? His understanding is inscrutable.

—Isaiah 40:28

Whoever hears these sayings of Mine and does them, I will liken him to a wise man who built his house on a rock. And the rain descended, the floods came, and the winds blew and beat on that house. And it did not fall, for it was founded a rock.

—MATTHEW 7:24–25

Then He said to them all, "If anyone will come after Me, let him deny himself, and take up his cross daily, and follow Me. For whoever will save his life will lose it, but whoever loses his life for My sake will save it."

—LUKE 9:23–24

Therefore let him who thinks he stands take heed, lest he fall. No temptation has taken you except what is common to man. God is faithful, and He will not permit you to be tempted above what you can endure, but will with the temptation also make a way to escape, that you may be able to bear it.

—1 CORINTHIANS 10:12–13

But, godliness with contentment is great gain. For we brought nothing into this world, and it is certain that we can carry nothing out. If we have food and clothing, we shall be content with these things.

—1 TIMOTHY 6:6–8

If any of you lacks wisdom, let him ask of God, who gives to all men liberally and without criticism, and it will be given to him.

—JAMES 1:5

BIBLICAL VALUES

But those things which proceed out of the mouth come from the heart, and they defile the man.

—MATTHEW 15:18

Jesus said to him, "'You shall love the Lord your God with all your heart, and with all your soul, and with all your mind.' This is the first and great commandment. And the second is like it: 'You shall love your neighbor as yourself.' On these two commandments hang all the Law and the Prophets."

—MATTHEW 22:37–40

I speak in human terms because of the weakness of your flesh, for just as you have yielded your members as slaves to impurity and iniquity leading to more iniquity, even so, now yield your members as slaves to righteousness unto holiness.

—ROMANS 6:19

Likewise, the Spirit helps us in our weaknesses, for we do not know what to pray for as we ought, but the Spirit

Himself intercedes for us with groanings too deep for words.

—ROMANS 8:26

We who are strong ought to bear the weaknesses of the weak and not please ourselves.

—ROMANS 15:1

No temptation has taken you except what is common to man. God is faithful, and He will not permit you to be tempted above what you can endure, but will with the temptation also make a way to escape, that you may be able to bear it.

—1 CORINTHIANS 10:13

For though He was crucified through weakness, yet He lives by the power of God. So also we are weak in Him, but we shall live with Him by the power of God serving you.

—2 CORINTHIANS 13:4

You, brothers, have been called to liberty. Only do not use liberty to give an opportunity to the flesh, but by love, serve one another. For the entire law is fulfilled in one word, even in this: "You shall love your neighbor as yourself."

—GALATIANS 5:13–14

And let us consider how to spur one another to love and to good works.

—Hebrews 10:24

God's Strength

The Lord is the strength of His people, and He is the saving strength of His anointed.

—Psalm 28:8

The Lord of Hosts is with us, the God of Jacob is our refuge.

—Psalm 46:11

That He would give you, according to the riches of His glory, power to be strengthened by His Spirit in the inner man, and that Christ may dwell in your hearts through faith; that you, being rooted and grounded in love.

—Ephesians 3:16–17

But He said to me, "My grace is sufficient for you, for My strength is made perfect in weakness." Therefore most gladly I will boast in my weaknesses, that the power of Christ may rest upon me.

—2 Corinthians 12:9

But the Lord stood with me and strengthened me, so that through me the preaching might be fully known, and that all the Gentiles might hear. And I was delivered out of the mouth of the lion. The Lord will deliver me from every evil work and will preserve me for His heavenly kingdom, to whom be glory forever and ever. Amen.

—2 TIMOTHY 4:17–18

GOD'S AUTHORITY

Do not judge according to appearance, but practice righteous judgment.

—JOHN 7:24

You judge according to the flesh. I judge no one. Yet if I do judge, My judgment is true. For I am not alone, but I am with the Father who sent Me.

—JOHN 8:15–16

The last enemy that will be destroyed is death.

—1 CORINTHIANS 15:26

When this corruptible will have put on incorruption, and this mortal will have put on immortality, then the saying that is written shall come to pass: "Death is swallowed up in victory." … The sting of death is sin, and the strength of sin is the law.

—1 CORINTHIANS 15:54, 56

For if a man with a gold ring, in fine clothing, comes into your assembly, and also a poor man in ragged clothing comes in, and you have respect for him who wears the fine clothing and say to him, "Sit here in a good place," and say to the poor, "Stand there," or "Sit here under my footstool," have you not then become partial among yourselves and become judges with evil thoughts?

—James 2:2–4

Experience Joy

The statutes of the Lord are right, rejoicing the heart. The commandment of the Lord is pure, enlightening the eyes.

—Psalm 19:8

For His anger endures but a moment, in His favor is life; weeping may endure for a night, but joy comes in the morning.

—Psalm 30:5

For our heart will rejoice in Him, because we have trusted in His holy name.

—Psalm 33:21

O come, let us sing unto the Lord; let us make a joyful noise to the rock of our salvation! Let us come before His presence with thanksgiving; let us make a joyful noise unto Him with psalms!

—Psalm 95:1–2

Make a joyful noise unto the Lord, all the earth! Serve the Lord with gladness; come before His presence with singing.

—Psalm 100:1–2

Blessed are the people who have such things; indeed, blessed are the people whose God is the Lord.

—Psalm 144:15

Sing, O heavens! And be joyful, O earth! And break forth into singing, O mountains! For the Lord has comforted His people and will have mercy on His afflicted.

—Isaiah 49:13

Therefore, the redeemed of the Lord shall return and come with singing to Zion. And everlasting joy shall be upon their head. They shall obtain gladness and joy. And sorrow and mourning shall flee away.

—Isaiah 51:11

Likewise, I tell you, there is joy in the presence of the angels of God over one sinner who repents.

—Luke 15:10

Until now you have asked nothing in My name. Ask, and you will receive, that your joy may be full.

—John 16:24

You have made known to me the ways of life. You will make me full of joy with Your presence.

—Acts 2:28

For the kingdom of God does not mean eating and drinking, but righteousness and peace and joy in the Holy Spirit.

—Romans 14:17

How in a great trial of affliction, the abundance of their joy and their deep poverty overflowed toward the riches of their generous giving.

—2 Corinthians 8:2

Rejoice in the Lord always. Again I will say, rejoice!

—Philippians 4:4

My brothers, count it all joy when you fall into diverse temptations, knowing that the trying of your faith develops patience.

—James 1:2–3

But rejoice in so far as you share in Christ's sufferings, so that you may rejoice and be glad also in the revelation of His glory.

—1 PETER 4:13

VICTORY IN SURRENDER

Not everyone who says to Me, "Lord, Lord," shall enter the kingdom of heaven, but he who does the will of My Father who is in heaven.

—MATTHEW 7:21

He went away a second time and prayed, "O My Father, if this cup may not pass away from Me unless I drink it, Your will be done."

—MATTHEW 26:42

I can do nothing of Myself. As I hear, I judge. My judgment is just, because I seek not My own will, but the will of the Father who sent Me.

—JOHN 5:30

He who has My commandments and keeps them is the one who loves Me. And he who loves Me will be loved by My Father. And I will love him and will reveal Myself to him.

—JOHN 14:21

"The opposite of sight and feeling is faith. Now it is the soulish person who gains assurance by grasping the things which can be seen and felt; but the person who follows the spirit lives by faith, not by sight."

WATCHMAN NEE

I urge you therefore, brothers, by the mercies of God, that you present your bodies as a living sacrifice, holy, and acceptable to God, which is your reasonable service of worship. Do not be conformed to this world, but be transformed by the renewing of your mind, that you may prove what is the good and acceptable and perfect will of God.

—ROMANS 12:1–2

You were bought with a price. Therefore glorify God in your body and in your spirit, which are God's.

—1 CORINTHIANS 6:20

Being submissive to one another in reverence for Christ.

—EPHESIANS 5:21

And being found in the form of a man, He humbled Himself and became obedient to death, even death on a cross. Therefore God highly exalted Him and gave Him the name which is above every name, that at the name of Jesus every knee should bow, of those in heaven and on earth and under the earth, and every tongue should confess that Jesus Christ is Lord, to the glory of God the Father.

—PHILIPPIANS 2:8–11

Therefore, my beloved, as you have always obeyed, not only in my presence, but so much more in my absence, work out your own salvation with fear and trembling. For God is

the One working in you, both to will and to do His good
pleasure.

—Philippians 2:12–13

As you have received Christ Jesus the Lord, so walk in Him,
rooted and built up in Him and established in the faith, as
you have been taught, and abounding with thanksgiving.

—Colossians 2:6–7

But, godliness with contentment is great gain.

—1 Timothy 6:6

All Scripture is inspired by God and is profitable for
teaching, for reproof, for correction, and for instruction in
righteousness, that the man of God may be complete, thoroughly equipped for every good work.

—2 Timothy 3:16–17

In the days of His flesh, Jesus offered up prayers and supplications with loud cries and tears to Him who was able to
save Him from death. He was heard because of His godly
fear. Though He was a Son, He learned obedience through
the things that He suffered.

—Hebrews 5:7–8

Let us look to Jesus, the author and finisher of our faith,
who for the joy that was set before Him endured the cross,

despising the shame, and is seated at the right hand of the throne of God. For consider Him who endured such hostility from sinners against Himself, lest you become weary and your hearts give up.

—HEBREWS 12:2–3

Submit yourselves to every human authority for the Lord's sake, whether it be to the king, as supreme, or to governors, who are sent by him for the punishment of evildoers and for the praise of those who do right. For it is the will of God that by doing right you may put to silence the ignorance of foolish men. As free people, do not use your liberty as a covering for evil, but live as servants of God.

—1 PETER 2:13–16

Chapter 8

PROMISES FOR LIVING IN VICTORY

REMAINING COMMITTED

For whoever would save his life will lose it, and whoever loses his life for My sake will find it.

—MATTHEW 16:25

Jesus said to him, "No one who put his hand to the plough and looks back at things is fit for the kingdom of God."

—LUKE 9:62

He who loves his life will lose it. And he who hates his life in this world will keep it for eternal life.

—JOHN 12:25

Remain in Me, as I also remain in you. As the branch cannot bear fruit by itself, unless it remains in the vine, neither can you, unless you remain in Me. I am the vine, you are the branches. He who remains in Me, and I in him, bears much fruit. For without Me you can do nothing.

—JOHN 15:4–5

But none of these things deter me. Nor do I count my life of value to myself, so that I may joyfully finish my course and the ministry which I have received from the Lord Jesus, to testify to the gospel of the grace of God.

—ACTS 20:24

No, in all these things we are more than conquerors through Him who loved us. I am persuaded that neither death nor life, neither angels nor principalities nor powers, neither things present nor things to come, neither height nor depth, nor any other created thing, shall be able to separate us from the love of God, which is in Christ Jesus our Lord.

—ROMANS 8:37–39

For if we live, we live for the Lord. And if we die, we die for the Lord. So, whether we live or die, we are the Lord's.

—ROMANS 14:8

Do you not know that all those who run in a race run, but one receives the prize? So run, that you may obtain it.

—1 CORINTHIANS 9:24

We are troubled on every side, yet not distressed; we are perplexed, but not in despair; persecuted, but not forsaken; cast down, but not destroyed; and always carrying around in the body the death of the Lord Jesus, that also the life of Jesus might be expressed in our bodies.

—2 CORINTHIANS 4:8–10

I have been crucified with Christ. It is no longer I who live, but Christ who lives in me. And the life I now live in the flesh, I live by faith in the Son of God, who loved me and gave Himself for me.

—Galatians 2:20

Yes, certainly, I count everything as loss for the excellence of the knowledge of Christ Jesus my Lord, for whom I have forfeited the loss of all things and count them as rubbish that I may gain Christ.

—Philippians 3:8

Brothers, I do not count myself to have attained, but this one thing I do, forgetting those things which are behind and reaching forward to those things which are ahead, I press toward the goal to the prize of the high calling of God in Christ Jesus.

—Philippians 3:13–14

And whatever you do, do it heartily, as to the Lord, and not for people, knowing that from the Lord you will receive the reward of the inheritance. For you serve the Lord Christ.

—Colossians 3:23–24

Learn to be calm, and to conduct your own business, and to work with your own hands, as we commanded you, so that you may walk honestly toward those who are outsiders and that you may lack nothing.

—1 Thessalonians 4:11–12

For God has not given us the spirit of fear, but of power, and love, and self-control.

—2 Timothy 1:7

Perseverance

The steps of a man are made firm by the Lord, he delights in His way. Though he falls, he will not be hurled down, for the Lord supports him with His hand.

—Psalm 37:23–24

Keep my commandments and live, and my teaching, as the apple of your eye.

—Proverbs 7:2

You will be hated by all men for My name's sake. But he who endures to the end will be saved.

—Matthew 10:22

We have diverse gifts according to the grace that is given to us: if prophecy, according to the proportion of faith; if service, in serving; he who teaches, in teaching; he who exhorts, in exhortation; he who gives, with generosity; he who rules, with diligence; he who shows mercy, with cheerfulness.

—ROMANS 12:6–8

Let all that you do be done with love.

—1 CORINTHIANS 16:14

Finally, my brothers, be strong in the Lord and in the power of His might.

—EPHESIANS 6:10

Therefore take up the whole armor of God that you may be able to resist in the evil day, and having done all, to stand. Stand therefore, having your waist girded with truth, having put on the breastplate of righteousness, having your feet fitted with the readiness of the gospel of peace.

—EPHESIANS 6:13–15

Set your affection on things above, not on things on earth.

—COLOSSIANS 3:2

Therefore we should be more attentive to what we have heard, lest we drift away.

—HEBREWS 2:1

But let patience perfect its work, that you may be perfect and complete, lacking nothing.

—JAMES 1:4

But whoever looks into the perfect law of liberty, and continues in it, and is not a forgetful hearer but a doer of the word, this man will be blessed in his deeds.

—JAMES 1:25

You therefore, beloved, since you know these things beforehand, beware lest you also fall from your own firm footing, being led away by the deception of the wicked. But grow in the grace and knowledge of our Lord and Savior Jesus Christ. To Him be glory, both now and forever. Amen.

—2 PETER 3:17–18

He who has an ear, let him hear what the Spirit says to the churches. To him who overcomes I will give permission to eat of the tree of life, which is in the midst of the Paradise of God.

—REVELATION 2:7

Do not fear any of those things which you are about to suffer. Look, the devil is about to throw some of you into prison, that you may be tried, and you will have tribulation for ten days. Be faithful unto death, and I will give you the crown of life.

—REVELATION 2:10

"He who is unjust, let him be unjust still. He who is filthy, let him be filthy still. He who is righteous, let him be righteous still. He who is holy, let him be holy still."

"Look, I am coming soon! My reward is with Me to give to each one according to his work."

—Revelation 22:11–12

Overcoming Pride

Lord, my heart is not haughty, my eyes are not raised too high. I have not striven for enormities, for things too wonderful for me.

—Psalm 131:1

When pride comes, then comes shame; but with the humble is wisdom.

—Proverbs 11:2

Do not labor to be rich; cease from your own wisdom. Will you set your eyes on that which is not? For riches certainly make themselves wings; they fly away as an eagle toward heaven.

—Proverbs 23:4–5

The end of a matter is better than the beginning of it, and the patient in spirit than the haughty in spirit.

—Ecclesiastes 7:8

Let nothing be done out of strife or conceit, but in humility let each esteem the other better than himself. Let each of you look not only to your own interests, but also to the interests of others. Let this mind be in you all, which was also in Christ Jesus.

—PHILIPPIANS 2:3–5

GETTING PAST FEAR

Be strong and of a good courage. Fear not, nor be afraid of them, for the LORD your God, it is He who goes with you. He will not fail you, nor forsake you.

—DEUTERONOMY 31:6

I lay down and slept; I awoke, for the LORD sustained me. I will not be afraid of multitudes of people who have set themselves against me round about.

—PSALM 3:5–6

The LORD is my light and my salvation; whom will I fear?

—PSALM 27:1

He gives power to the faint, and to those who have no might He increases strength. Even the youths shall faint and be weary, and the young men shall utterly fall. But those who wait upon the LORD shall renew their strength. They shall mount up with wings as eagles. They shall run, and not be weary. And they shall walk, and not faint.

—ISAIAH 40:29–31

Do not fear, for I am with you. Do not be dismayed, for I am your God. I will strengthen you. Indeed, I will help you. Indeed, I will uphold you with My righteous right hand.

—Isaiah 41:10

Grieving the Loss of a Loved One

The eye of the Lord is on those who fear Him, on those who hope in His lovingkindness, to deliver their soul from death, and to keep them alive in famine. Our soul waits for the Lord; He is our help and our shield.

—Psalm 33:18–20

Blessed are those who mourn, for they shall be comforted.

—Matthew 5:4

And if Christ is in you, though the body is dead because of sin, the Spirit is alive because of righteousness. But if the Spirit of Him who raised Jesus from the dead lives in you, He who raised Christ from the dead will also give life to your mortal bodies through His Spirit that lives in you.

—Romans 8:10–11

For none of us lives for himself, and no one dies for himself. For if we live, we live for the Lord. And if we die, we die for the Lord. So, whether we live or die, we are the Lord's.

—Romans 14:7–8

For to me, to continue living is Christ, and to die is gain.

—PHILIPPIANS 1:21

FINDING PEACE IN THE STORM

The LORD your God will restore your fortunes and have compassion on you. He will assemble you again, from all the nations to which the LORD your God scattered you.

—DEUTERONOMY 30:3

In You, O LORD, I seek refuge; may I never be put to shame. Deliver me in Your righteousness and help me escape; incline Your ear to me and save me.... For You are my hope, O LORD God; You are my confidence from my youth.

—PSALM 71:1–2, 5

O come, let us worship and bow down; let us kneel before the LORD, our Maker. For He is our God, and we are the people of His pasture and the sheep of His hand. Today if you hear His voice, do not harden your hearts, as at Meribah, and as in the day of Massah in the wilderness.

—PSALM 95:6–8

To the upright there arises light in the darkness; he is gracious, and full of compassion, and righteous.

—PSALM 112:4

Our help is in the name of the Lord, who made heaven and earth.

—Psalm 124:8

Blessed is the one who has the God of Jacob for his help, whose hope is in the Lord his God.

—Psalm 146:5

He has made everything beautiful in its appropriate time. He has also put obscurity in their hearts so that people do not come to know the work that God has done from the beginning to the end. I experienced that there is nothing better for people than to be glad and do good in their life.

—Ecclesiastes 3:11–12

You will keep him in perfect peace, whose mind is stayed on You, because he trusts in You.

—Isaiah 26:3

Even the youths shall faint and be weary, and the young men shall utterly fall. But those who wait upon the Lord shall renew their strength. They shall mount up with wings as eagles. They shall run, and not be weary. And they shall walk, and not faint.

—Isaiah 40:30–31

But now, thus says the Lord who created you, O Jacob, and He who formed you, O Israel, "Do not fear, for I have redeemed you. I have called you by your name. You are Mine."

—Isaiah 43:1

PATIENCE

Rest in the LORD, and wait patiently for Him; do not fret because of those who prosper in their way, because of those who make wicked schemes.

—Psalm 37:7

To those who by patiently doing good seek for glory and honor and immortality, will be eternal life.

—Romans 2:7

Not only so, but we also boast in tribulation, knowing that tribulation produces patience, patience produces character, and character produces hope. And hope does not disappoint, because the love of God is shed abroad in our hearts by the Holy Spirit who has been given to us.

—Romans 5:3–5

Indeed, we told you before when we were with you that we would suffer tribulation, just as it came to pass, as you well know. For this reason, when I could no longer endure it, I sent to inquire about your faith, lest by some means the tempter might have tempted you, and our labor might have been in vain.

—1 THESSALONIANS 3:4–5

Now we exhort you, brothers, warn those who are unruly, comfort the faint-hearted, support the weak, and be patient toward everyone.

—1 THESSALONIANS 5:14

For you need patience, so that after you have done the will of God, you will receive the promise.

—HEBREWS 10:36

Therefore, since we are encompassed with such a great cloud of witnesses, let us also lay aside every weight and the sin that so easily entangles us, and let us run with endurance the race that is set before us. Let us look to Jesus, the author and finisher of our faith, who for the joy that was set before Him endured the cross, despising the shame, and is seated at the right hand of the throne of God.

—HEBREWS 12:1–2

Therefore, my beloved brothers, let every man be swift to hear, slow to speak, and slow to anger, for the anger of man does not work the righteousness of God.

—JAMES 1:19–20

The Lord is not slow concerning His promise, as some count slowness. But He is patient with us, because He does not want any to perish, but all to come to repentance.

—2 Peter 3:9

Loving God

I love You, O Lord, my strength. The Lord is my pillar, and my fortress, and my deliverer; my God, my rock, in whom I take refuge; my shield, and the horn of my salvation, my high tower.

—Psalm 18:1–2

Blessed be the Lord my strength, who prepares my hands for war, and my fingers to fight; my goodness, and my fortress; my high tower, and my deliverer, my shield, and in whom I trust; who subdues nations under me.

—Psalm 144:1–2

Jesus answered him, "The first of all the commandments is, 'Hear, O Israel, the Lord our God is one Lord. You shall love the Lord your God with all your heart, and with all your soul, and with all your mind, and with all your strength.' This is the first commandment."

—Mark 12:29–30

To love Him with all the heart, and with all the understanding, and with all the soul, and with all the strength, and to love one's neighbor as oneself, is more than all burnt offerings and sacrifices.

—MARK 12:33

Jesus said to them, "If God were your Father, you would love Me, for I came from God and proceeded into the world. I did not come of My own authority, but He sent Me."

—JOHN 8:42

If you love Me, keep My commandments....He who has My commandments and keeps them is the one who loves Me. And he who loves Me will be loved by My Father. And I will love him and will reveal Myself to him.

—JOHN 14:15, 21

We know that all things work together for good to those who love God, to those who are called according to His purpose.

—ROMANS 8:28

But if anyone loves God, this one is known by Him.

—1 CORINTHIANS 8:3

There is no fear in love, but perfect love casts out fear, because fear has to do with punishment. Whoever fears is not perfect in love. We love Him because He first loved us. If anyone says, "I love God," and hates his brother, he is a liar. For whoever does not love his brother whom he has seen, how can he love God whom he has not seen? We have this commandment from Him: Whoever loves God must also love his brother.

—1 JOHN 4:18–20

KNOWING JESUS

Then Jesus came and spoke to them saying, "All authority has been given to Me in heaven and on earth."

—MATTHEW 28:18

For God did not send His Son into the world to condemn the world, but that the world through Him might be saved.

—JOHN 3:17

For the wages of sin is death, but the gift of God is eternal life through Jesus Christ our Lord.

—ROMANS 6:23

But thanks be to God, who gives us the victory through our Lord Jesus Christ!

—1 CORINTHIANS 15:57

Knowing that He who raised the Lord Jesus will also raise us through Jesus and will present us with you.

—2 CORINTHIANS 4:14

Therefore God highly exalted Him and gave Him the name which is above every name, that at the name of Jesus every knee should bow, of those in heaven and on earth and under the earth, and every tongue should confess that Jesus Christ is Lord, to the glory of God the Father.

—Philippians 2:9–11

For if we believe that Jesus died and arose again, so God will bring with Him those who sleep in Jesus.

—1 Thessalonians 4:14

But I received mercy for this reason, that in me, first, Jesus Christ might show all patience, as an example to those who were to believe in Him for eternal life. Now to the eternal, immortal, invisible King, the only wise God, be honor and glory forever. Amen.

—1 Timothy 1:16–17

And we have seen and testify that the Father sent the Son to be the Savior of the world.

—1 John 4:14

He said to me, "It is done. I am the Alpha and the Omega, the Beginning and the End. I will give of the spring of the water of life to him who thirsts. He who overcomes shall inherit all things, and I will be his God and he shall be My son."

—Revelation 21:6–7

FOLLOWING JESUS

You are the light of the world. A city that is set on a hill cannot be hidden. Neither do men light a candle and put it under a basket, but on a candlestick. And it gives light to all who are in the house. Let your light so shine before men that they may see your good works and glorify your Father who is in heaven.

—MATTHEW 5:14–16

Therefore, since we have been justified by faith, we have peace with God through our Lord Jesus Christ, through whom we also have access by faith into this grace in which we stand, and so we rejoice in hope of the glory of God. Not only so, but we also boast in tribulation, knowing that tribulation produces patience, patience produces character, and character produces hope.

—ROMANS 5:1–4

We have such trust through Christ toward God, not that we are sufficient in ourselves to take credit for anything of ourselves, but our sufficiency is from God.

—2 CORINTHIANS 3:4–5

Until we all come into the unity of the faith and of the knowledge of the Son of God, into a complete man, to the measure of the stature of the fullness of Christ.

—EPHESIANS 4:13

Finally, my brothers, be strong in the Lord and in the power of His might. Put on the whole armor of God that you may be able to stand against the schemes of the devil.

—Ephesians 6:10–11

For in Him lives all the fullness of the Godhead bodily. And you are complete in Him, who is the head of all authority and power.

—Colossians 2:9–10

Let the word of Christ dwell in you richly in all wisdom, teaching and admonishing one another in psalms and hymns and spiritual songs, singing with grace in your hearts to the Lord. And whatever you do in word or deed, do all in the name of the Lord Jesus, giving thanks to God the Father through Him.

—Colossians 3:16–17

Command those who are rich in this world that they not be conceited, nor trust in uncertain riches, but in the living God, who richly gives us all things to enjoy. Command that they do good, that they be rich in good works, generous, willing to share, and laying up in store for themselves a good foundation for the coming age, so that they may take hold of eternal life.

—1 Timothy 6:17–19

We all err in many ways. But if any man does not err in word, he is a perfect man and able also to control the whole body.

—JAMES 3:2

If anyone speaks, let him speak as the oracles of God. If anyone serves, let him serve with the strength that God supplies, so that God in all things may be glorified through Jesus Christ, to whom be praise and dominion forever and ever. Amen.

—1 PETER 4:11

By this we know that we know Him, if we keep His commandments. Whoever says, "I know Him," and does not keep His commandments is a liar, and the truth is not in him. But whoever keeps His word truly has the love of God perfected in him. By this we know we are in Him.

—1 JOHN 2:3–5

My little children, let us love not in word and speech, but in action and truth.

—1 JOHN 3:18

For whoever is born of God overcomes the world, and the victory that overcomes the world is our faith. Who is it that overcomes the world, but the one who believes that Jesus is the Son of God?

—1 JOHN 5:4–5

The Power of the Tongue

Lord, who will abide in Your tabernacle? Who will dwell in Your holy hill? He who walks uprightly, and does righteousness, and speaks truth in his own heart. He who does not slander with the tongue, nor does evil to his neighbor, nor bears a reproach against a person close by. In whose eyes a vile person is despised, but he honors those who fear the Lord, he swears to avoid evil and does not change.

—Psalm 15:1–4

The mouth of the righteous utters wisdom, and their tongue speaks justice. The law of their God is in their heart; none of their steps will slip.

—Psalm 37:30–31

He who is void of wisdom despises his neighbor, but a man of understanding holds his peace. A talebearer reveals secrets, but he who is of a faithful spirit conceals the matter.

—Proverbs 11:12–13

A man will be satisfied with good by the fruit of his mouth, and the recompense of a man's hands will be rendered to him.

—Proverbs 12:14

There is one who speaks like the piercings of a sword, but the tongue of the wise is health. The truthful lip will be established forever, but a lying tongue is but for a moment.

—Proverbs 12:18–19

Lying lips are an abomination to the Lord, but those who deal truly are His delight. A prudent man conceals knowledge, but the heart of fools proclaims foolishness.

—Proverbs 12:22–23

He who guards his mouth preserves his life, but he who opens his lips will have destruction.

—Proverbs 13:3

A perverse man sows strife, and a whisperer separates the best of friends.

—Proverbs 16:28

Death and life are in the power of the tongue, and those who love it will eat its fruit.

—Proverbs 18:21

O generation of vipers, how can you, being evil, speak good things? For out of the abundance of the heart the mouth speaks.

—Matthew 12:34

Let no unwholesome word proceed out of your mouth, but only that which is good for building up, that it may give grace to the listeners.

—Ephesians 4:29

If anyone among you seems to be religious and does not bridle his tongue, but deceives his own heart, this man's religion is vain.

—James 1:26

With it we bless the Lord and Father, and with it we curse men, who are made in the image of God. Out of the same mouth proceed blessing and cursing. My brothers, these things ought not to be so.

—James 3:9–10

For "He who wants to love life, and to see good days, let him keep his tongue from evil, and his lips from speaking deceit. Let him turn away from evil and do good. Let him seek peace and pursue it."

—1 Peter 3:10–11

Give Thanks to God

For You have turned my mourning into dancing; You have put off my sackcloth and girded me with gladness, so that my glory may sing praise to You and not be silent. O LORD my God, I will give thanks to You forever.

—PSALM 30:11–12

Now thanks be to God who always causes us to triumph in Christ and through us reveals the fragrance of His knowledge in every place. For we are to God a sweet fragrance of Christ among those who are saved and among those who perish.

—2 CORINTHIANS 2:14–15

Do not cease giving thanks for you, mentioning you in my prayers, so that the God of our Lord Jesus Christ, the Father of glory, may give you the Spirit of wisdom and revelation in the knowledge of Him.

—EPHESIANS 1:16–17

Speak to one another in psalms, hymns and spiritual songs, singing and making melody in your heart to the Lord. Give thanks always for all things to God the Father in the name of our Lord Jesus Christ.

—EPHESIANS 5:19–20

And whatever you do in word or deed, do all in the name of the Lord Jesus, giving thanks to God the Father through Him.

—COLOSSIANS 3:17

In everything give thanks, for this is the will of God in Christ Jesus concerning you.

—1 Thessalonians 5:18

Therefore, since we are receiving a kingdom that cannot be moved, let us be gracious, by which we may serve God acceptably with reverence and godly fear.

—Hebrews 12:28

Through Him, then, let us continually offer to God the sacrifice of praise, which is the fruit of our lips, giving thanks to His name.

—Hebrews 13:15

We give You thanks, O Lord God Almighty, who is and was and who is to come, because You have taken Your great power and reign.

—Revelation 11:17

Blessing and glory and wisdom and thanksgiving and honor and power and might be to our God forever and ever!

—Revelation 7:12

FREE NEWSLETTERS
TO HELP EMPOWER YOUR LIFE

Why subscribe today?

❏ **DELIVERED DIRECTLY TO YOU.** All you have to do is open your inbox and read.

❏ **EXCLUSIVE CONTENT.** We cover the news overlooked by the mainstream press.

❏ **STAY CURRENT.** Find the latest court rulings, revivals, and cultural trends.

❏ **UPDATE OTHERS.** Easy to forward to friends and family with the click of your mouse.

CHOOSE THE E-NEWSLETTER THAT INTERESTS YOU MOST:

- Christian news
- Daily devotionals
- Spiritual empowerment
- And much, much more

SIGN UP AT: **http://freenewsletters.charismamag.com**